D1716039

BRITISH **ART
DEC
O** CERAMICS

British *ART*
DECO *Ceramics*

Colin Mawston

Schiffer Publishing Ltd®

4880 Lower Valley Road, Atglen, PA 19310 USA

East Baton Rouge Parish Library
Baton Rouge, Louisiana

DEDICATION

This book is dedicated to Hannah and William.
For their knowledge and enthusiasm of the subject
they know is my passion.
In the hope that they will become the next guard-
ians of my collection, and for just being my children.

PRICES

Prices quoted in this book are based on dealers' prices in conjunction with dealers' and collectors' views and auction results. They are made on the assumption that items are in pristine condition and are readily available on an open market. Depending on the circumstances of a transaction, prices can vary significantly. You will,

undoubtably, encounter bargains and conversely, certain pieces will exceed expected prices.

The prices given, therefore, should be regarded as a very general guide and not prescriptive. At the end of the day, purchasers have to decide what the value of particular items are to themselves.

Whilst every care has been exercised in the compilation of this book, neither the author or publisher accept any liability for any financial loss incurred by reliance placed on the information contained herein.

Editor's Note: Numerous British spellings are in use throughout this manuscript.

Copyright © 2000 by Colin Mawston

Library of Congress
Cataloging-in -Publication Data

Mawston, Colin.
British art deco ceramics / Colin Mawston.
   p. cm.
Includes bibliographical references.
ISBN 0-7643-1059-3
   1. Pottery, British. 2. Pottery--20th century--Great Britain. 3. Decoration and ornament--Great Britain--Art Deco. I. Title.

NK4085.M38 2000
738'.0941'09041--dc21
                              99-054505

Clarice Cliff and Susie Cooper Designs and backstamps reproduced with kind permission of Josiah Wedgwood & Sons Limited, owners of the registered trade marks of "Clarice Cliff" and "Bizarre."

All rights reserved. No part of this work may be reproduced or used in any form or by any means—graphic, electronic, or mechanical, including photocopying or information storage and retrieval systems—without written permission from the copyright holder.
"Schiffer," "Schiffer Publishing Ltd. & Design," and the "Design of pen and ink well" are registered trademarks of Schiffer Publishing Ltd.

Cover design by Bruce Waters
Book design by Blair Loughrey
Type set in Albertus medium/Zurich/Zapf Humanist /Dutch 801 Rm BT/Rage Italic

ISBN: 0-7643-1059-3
Printed in China

We are interested in hearing from authors with book ideas on related subjects.

Published by Schiffer Publishing Ltd.
4880 Lower Valley Road
Atglen, PA 19310
Phone: (610) 593-1777; Fax: (610) 593-2002
E-mail: Schifferbk@aol.com
Please visit our web site catalog at
WWW.SCHIFFERBOOKS.COM
or write for a free catalog.
This book may be purchased from the publisher.
Please include $3.95 for shipping.

In Europe, Schiffer books are distributed by
Bushwood Books
6 Marksbury Ave.
Kew Gardens
Surrey TW9 4JF England
Phone: 44 (0)208 392-8585
Fax: 44 (0)208 392-9876
E-mail: Bushwd@aol.com
Free postage in the UK. Europe: air mail at cost
Please try your bookstore first.

CONTENTS

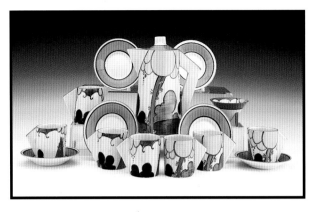

ACKNOWLEDGMENTS

Book writing is made more pleasurable by the many people encountered along the way. With a few notable exceptions, the enthusiasm and helpfulness of those individuals has been overwhelming; without them, this book would not have been possible.

Thank you to Eric Knowles of Bonhams, for his words of encouragement and for supplying photographs for the book.

My appreciation to Lyn Miller of the Wedgwood Museum, Julie McKeown of the Sir Henry Doulton Gallery and Alice Whitehead of the Bridgeman Art Library for their kindness and assistance.

I am also very grateful to Harry of New Century and Andrew Carew-Cox for their help with the Dr. Chr. Dresser photographs.

Undoubtedly, one of the greatest pleasures of the venture was being invited by Jonathan and Alan, of Banana Dance, to photograph their private collection of Clarice Cliff. Many items from their collection are featured in this book and I am grateful to them for providing that opportunity.

The process of writing a book is a learning experience for the writer and I am most obliged to all the experts, collectors, and other authors who have shared their knowledge with me. Thank you to Elizabeth Coupe and her husband for their help with the Burleigh Ware text and for supplying photographs. To Andrew Casey, for his help and assistance with the Susie Cooper text. To Dr. Phil Woodward, Len Griffin, and Andrew Hutton for their help and suggestions relating to the Clarice Cliff chapter. To Chris Davenport, for his advice in respect of Shelley. To Helen Calvert, for help and for supplying photos of Chameleon Ware.

The most pleasant surprise, whilst writing the book, has been the discovery that Eddie Sadler, the designer of the Racing Car Teapot, is alive and well and actually still working for James Sadler. Thank you, Eddie and Richard Eagleton, for providing material and information.

The writing of this book has enabled me to make many new acquaintances and through the wonder of the internet, distance has been cast aside. Thank you to Carole Berk in the States and to Keiko Okabe in Japan for your kind assistance.

A special thanks to Helen and Keith Martin of Carlton Ware Collectors International for their help with the Carlton Ware chapter and for their wonderful response to my plea for photographs.

Thanks also to Jonathan Brough of Bona Arts, Lindsey Drewett and Chris Parker of Sothebys, Harold and Maureen, John Bingham, Alison Dobbs, Ian Prince, and John Murray.

I would also like to thank my wife, Susan, and my children, Hannah and William, for their support through the enforced period of alienation that this book has demanded and for their help with technical matters.

Finally, this book would not have been possible without the patience and enthusiasm of Bernard Farrant, who took all the photographs, except where stated.

Chapter 1

INTRODUCTION TO ART DECO

The term Art Deco is taken from the name of an exhibition called "L'Exposition Internationale des Arts Decoratifs et Industriels Modernes," held in Paris in 1925. However, the term was not actually used until the mid-1960s, when it was referred to in newspaper articles and the Bevis Hillier book "Art Deco."[1]

In its own time, Art Deco was known by many different names including Art Moderne, Style Moderne, and Jazz Age. At that time, there were many conflicts between the various styles. The Modernists decried any form of decoration to objects. Whereas, the French Traditionalists (e.g.Ruhlman and Lalique) took a polarized view and feasted on decoration. Other movements married the opposing views. It would not have been possible at the time to label the various styles under one heading. However, sitting back today and peering over the

time gap of seventy years or so, it is generally acceptable to most enthusiasts of the era to group all the strands and styles under the general heading of Art Deco.

A simple suggested definition is that it is "the artistic style of the 1920s and 1930s." Although, that is not to say, that everything produced in that time is Art Deco. Many companies hung on to the past and their products, whilst being produced in the era, owe nothing to Art Deco. Some of the British potteries were firmly rooted in previous styles and continued, throughout the 1920s and 1930s, to produce pottery reflecting Art Nouveau and the Arts and Crafts movements.

The myth that anything produced in the era is Art Deco is perpetuated by some books, mixing Art Nouveau, Arts and Crafts, and Art Deco indiscriminately.

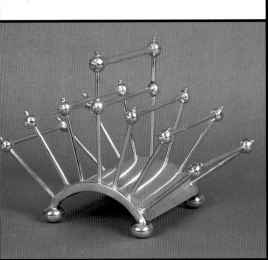

Toast Rack with balls at intersecting angles, designed by Dr. Christopher Dresser for Hukin & Heath, c. 1881. *Photograph by Alastair Carew-Cox and courtesy of New Century.* $1500.

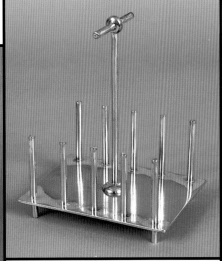

Toast Rack designed by Dr. Chr. Dresser for Hukin & Heath, c. 1878. Despite being produced over forty years prior to the Deco era, this toastrack could very easily be mistaken as being from the period. *Photograph by Alastair Carew-Cox and courtesy of New Century.* $4000.

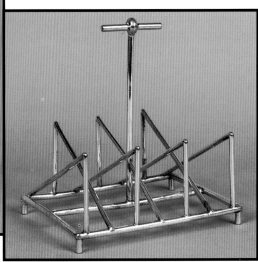

Decades ahead of its time, a very simple and stylish Toast Rack designed by Dr. Chr. Dresser for Dixons, c. 1879. *Photograph by Alastair Carew-Cox and courtesy of New Century.* $7500.

ORIGINS OF ART DECO

The "official" time period of Art Deco is the years between the end of the first world war and the beginning of the second world war. And, to fit neatly into the pigeon holes of time, it is said to immediately follow the previous art style of Art Nouveau. However, its origins can be traced back to many years before that time.

One of the forefathers of Art Deco is, undoubtedly, Dr. Christopher Dresser (1834-1904). Born in Scotland and trained as a botanist, Dr. Dresser was the first modern product designer. He foresaw, as early as 1850, that designs could only reach a large market at a low price through industry. He advocated that beauty and utility should be combined and that mass production necessitated a new approach to design. Dresser worked in many mediums, including metal and ceramics. His metal teapots, toast racks, and chambersticks shout Art Deco, even though they were made fifty years prior to the era. He was also the art director of the Linthorpe pottery (1879-1882), were he introduced cups with triangular handles that had a distinct deco look

The work of the Scottish architect, Charles Rennie Mackintosh (1868-1928), was to have a profound effect and influence on Art Deco. Whereas, he is principally associated with Art Nouveau, Mackintosh integrated distinct Art Deco looks in his furniture and poster designs.

Whereas, most of the pioneers of Art Deco were to be found in Europe, the United States, through the work of Frank Lloyd Wright (1867-1959), was a major player in its development. Although principally an architect, he believed that a building should be considered as a whole entity, including the interior, furnishings and decorations. In pursuit of integration, Wright designed many things, including leaded glass windows based on geometrics, and introduced metal furniture as early as 1904. He also designed innovative ceramics for the Imperial hotel Tokyo in 1915, that utilised a stark white background with perhaps the first psychedelic pattern ever used.

Sharing the ideals of Frank Lloyd Wright and influenced by Mackintosh, the Austrian designer Joseph Hoffman (1870-1956) became a major shaper of the forthcoming Art Deco style. He designed buildings, furniture, glass, metalwork, and ceramics. In 1903, Hoffman founded the Wiener Werkstätte (the Vienna workshops) with the intention of producing simple, high quality items for the home.

In 1919, Walter Gropius (1883-1969) formed the Bauhaus. This was an art school in Germany that believed designers should be trained to work with industry and promoted the principle of "form follows function."

Other influential groups included the Dutch De Stijl movement (the Style). This included members such as Piet Mondrian, whose cubist painting was to influence Clarice Cliff, and Gerrit Rietveld, whose Red/Blue chair of 1918 is generally recognised as an icon of Moderne design.

There is no doubt that the 1925 Paris exhibition was a showcase for Art Deco. It was an international affair and the brief from the organisers to exhibitors was to show products that did not copy previous styles. More than 20 different countries exhibited, with notable exceptions being Germany (for political reasons) and the USA.

Although the USA did not exhibit, it did send representatives from the Department of Commerce. They noted that the style of the exhibition would give a major competitive advantage to countries integrating that style into production items. However, the exhibition was heavily subsidised by the French (who occupied the majority of the site) and was used by them as a vehicle to promote French interests and to beat off German/Austrian competition.

Left: A Jug designed by Dr. Chr. Dresser for Linthorpe Pottery. 8.5 inches high, c. 1879. *Photograph by Alastair Carew-Cox and courtesy of New Century.* $4000.

Lower left: A Chamber Stick by Hukin and Heath attributed to Dr. Christopher Dresser. *Courtesy of Decodance.* $650.

Below: A covered box/jar showing a design by Frank Lloyd Wright for the Hotel Imperial Tokyo in 1915. It was later re-issued by Tiffany. *Courtesy of Decodance.* NP

INFLUENCES ON ART DECO

During World War One, the people of the west had suffered untold misery. At the end of the hostilities in 1919, there was a general move towards a new beginning. The greyness of life during the war was replaced with a desire for color and a celebration of life itself. This opened the door for Art Deco and the roaring twenties was unleashed.

The role of women changed dramatically. Many women had taken over the jobs of men during the war. This, together with the suffragette movement, placed women in a different light. During the Art Nouveau period, women had been portrayed as subservient maidens. Now they were featured in posters and bronzes smoking, driving, drinking, and pursuing sporting activities.

A major influence for Art Deco was the Performing Arts. As well as spawning thousands of Art Deco inspired cinemas, the movies brought style into the lives of millions of people. The silver screen introduced ordinary people to fashion and design and they became conscious of those attributes. Stage productions such as the Ballet Russe in Paris introduced audiences to the costumes and set designs of Erté.

When Josephine Baker appeared in La Revue Negre in 1925, negro art and culture was featured and jazz dancing became a feature of the deco era.

During the inter-war years, there was a fascination with speed. World records for land, sea, and air were broken and this encouraged streamlined products. The discovery of Tutankhamen's tomb in 1922 influenced Art Deco design, particularly in respect to jewelry.

However, by far the greatest influence on Art Deco was the advance in industry and technology. The deco period coincided with the machine age. This meant that items could be mass produced if they were designed with industry in mind. Consequently, the flowing curvilinear lines of Art Nouveau were rejected and replaced with industry friendly streamlined, angular, and geometric forms. The rapid advances in technology also brought new materials, such as Bakelite and chrome, which had a major effect on the product style.

In some respects, Art Deco can be seen as a contrary reaction to Art Nouveau. Certainly, the fussiness and gratuitous decoration of the Nouveau style is frequently displaced by the spirit of Deco. However, the two styles do have many things in common. They both exude an element of freedom of expression and many of the motifs and subjects of Nouveau are carried into the Deco style. In the field of ceramics, the colorful glazes of Minton Pottery laid the groundwork of what was to follow. And the Tube Lining and Outlining techniques they used would be later utilized by Charlotte Rhead and Clarice Cliff respectively.

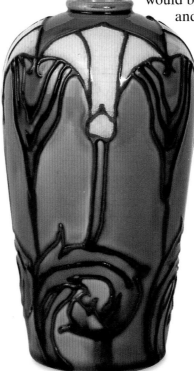

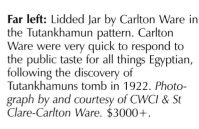

Far left: Lidded Jar by Carlton Ware in the Tutankhamun pattern. Carlton Ware were very quick to respond to the public taste for all things Egyptian, following the discovery of Tutankhamuns tomb in 1922. *Photograph by and courtesy of CWCI & St Clare-Carlton Ware.* $3000+.

Left: Vase by Minton, 5.5 inches high, c. 1905. From the Art Nouveau period. Whereas the curvilinear decoration would soon give way to geometric forms, it does lay the ground for intensely colored patterns. The use of tube lining, as featured here, was also developed in later years by Charlotte Rhead and Moorcroft. *Courtesy of Decodance.* $320.

A TOTAL STYLE

Prior to Art Deco, art and style were generally limited to specific items and only available to the very rich. The rising middle class combined with heightened industrial production increased both the demand for, and availability of, such wares gigantically.

Whereas, the era witnessed great economic depression, it did in general see a rise in living standards and the creation of a new middle class. This gave birth to new mass markets and industry, through mass production was able to deliver the required style and design at the right price.

Through new mass communications media (newspapers, telephone, radio, and the cinema), Art Deco was embraced by numerous countries and became an international style. The era coincided with a worldwide building program and many new buildings, particularly in the USA, exuded Art Deco. Together with architecture, the style embraced all conceivable areas including ceramics, painting, metalwork, glass, furniture, jewelry, advertising, and furniture.

Mass demand, and the ability of industry to oblige, also meant that style was injected, for the first time, into an enormous spread of items that had hitherto not been subjected to style, including household appliances and the most mundane of items.

Art Deco is a style derived from a period of rapid change and unique circumstances. It could be said that it was in the right place at the right time. As suggested by Bevis Hillier in his book *Art Deco*, and later restated by him and Stephen Escritt in their book *Art Deco Style*, Art Deco is a "Total Style".[2] It is undoubtedly the first ever "Total Style," and quite possibly the last.

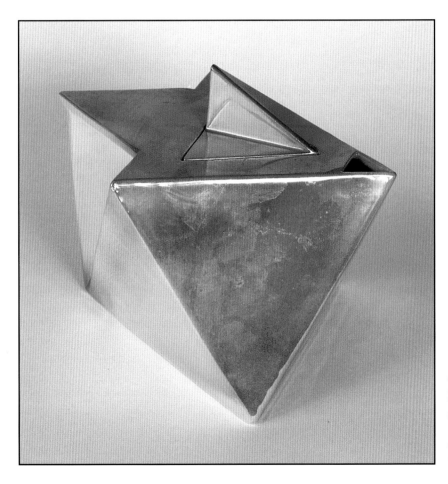

An unusual and extremely designed Teapot "Art Deco Meets the Space Age." Maker unknown. *Courtesy of Decodance.* NP (**N**o **P**rice)

THE CONTRIBUTION OF BRITISH

Chapter 2

ART DECO CERAMICS

Vases and Jugs by Clarice Cliff. Top Row: Original Bizarre, Rudyard, Berries, Orange Lily, and Original Bizarre. Middle Row: Original Bizarre, Forest Glen Tube Vase, Forest Glen Wall Plate, Coral firs, and Delecia Citrus. Bottom Row: Summerhouse, Inspiration Caprice, Original Bizarre and Poplar. *Photograph by and Courtesy of Carole A Berk Ltd.* $1500-6000+.

The pottery industry in Britain during the inter-war years was generally based in the county of Staffordshire in the Midlands area of the country (a notable exception being Poole Pottery in Dorset). This area was and is still known as "the Potteries" and included the north Staffordshire towns of Tunstall, Burslem, Hanley, Fenton, and Longton. All of these towns are within a few miles of each other and their primary industry in the deco era was the production of pottery.

The area has a long history of pottery production, going back to before Roman times. The first recorded pottery factory was established in the seventeenth century. The historical reason behind the siting of the industry was the local availability of the bare essentials of the industry—coal, clay, water, and skilled labour.

At the beginning of the twentieth century, the potteries produced unimaginative traditional shapes and patterns. It was not until the late 1920s that the industry woke up to the requirement of a new order. However, once awakened, the potteries pursued the new styles with a vengeance and brought color and style into millions of homes.

During the inter-war years, there were as many as 400 different factories in the area, all of which were generally "family owned." There was a great sense of competition between the factories and they were all eager to introduce new lines to gain market shares. Undoubtedly, much of the output of the pottery companies was very similar in concept, pattern, and design. Many times, I have glanced at an item and thought that it was a piece of early Grays, only to discover on closer inspection that it was in fact from the Crown Devon factory. The reason why shapes are common to different companies is that many shared the same supplier of undecorated blank pottery. Although, some factories (e.g. Carlton Ware and Crown Devon) shared the same designers, in many cases the similarity of patterns is probably nothing more than plagiarism.

The industry had its own trade journal called *The Pottery Gazette and Glass Trade Review,* which attempted to give a common voice and constantly warned of the threat from foreign imports, particularily from Japan and Czechoslovakia. Accompanying a strong home market trade, the potteries successfully exported to many countries including Australia, New Zealand, South Africa, Canada, and North America. Even at the outbreak of World War Two, when the British government banned the hand-painting of ceramics, an exception was made for exports, in view of the industries capacity to earn much needed foreign currency.

It has been suggested by some writers that British Art Deco ceramics are the poor relations of some other producing countries. Despite the cynicism of some academics, it is suggested that none would now argue that the most famous and successful of all Art Deco ceramic designers, both then and now, is the British designer Clarice Cliff. To some, her work was flashy. I respond to that by saying that they do not fully understand her work and would invite them to consider that the hand-painted decoration of her work is perhaps the nearest you will ever get to art on widely available pottery.

Above: Czechoslovakian Vases by Ditmar Urbach. The British pottery industry was constantly under threat from foreign imports, principally from Japan and Czechoslovakia. *Courtesy of Decodance.* $350 each.

Left: A selection of various shapes and patterns by Clarice Cliff. *Photograph by and Courtesy of Carole A Berk Ltd.* $650-3000+.

A problem suffered by British Art Deco ceramics, has been the inaccurate information provided by some of the early writers on the subject. In her book *Art Deco A Guide For Collectors,*[1] Katharine Morrison McClinton, stated that Clarice Cliff designed two patterns, one called "Bizarre" and the other "Fantasque." We now know that these are not patterns, but ranges of patterns. In fact, Clarice Cliff was responsible for designing over 750 new shapes and 500 patterns. Her "Bizarre" range alone produced 8.5 million sales in less than ten years.

Whereas it is accepted that the output of the Staffordshire Potteries was indeed directed at a much wider market than the elitist products of some countries, it is this very factor which gives British Art Deco ceramics the honour of being among the greatest contributors to the total Art Deco style. Prior, to the Art Deco age, art or style was the exclusive province of the very rich. The marketing and production techniques of the British potteries went a long way to change that and made the Art Deco style available for all. Even so, not all the British products were cheap. Some of the ranges from Clarice Cliff and the Shelley Potteries were, in particular, quite expensive and the usual places of their purchase was from stores such as Harrods and Lawleys. The majority of purchasers were probably from the rising middle classes. Although, less well off customers would also acquire the pottery as wedding gifts or bottom draw acquisitions.

A further contribution of the British Potteries was the extent to which women were encouraged to participate and take a leading role. The early part of the twentieth century was undoubtedly a man's world. Yet, the most famous of the British Art Deco potters are all women—Clarice Cliff, Susie Cooper, and Charlotte Rhead. A particularly effective marketing tool of the British companies was to create designer labels. All Clarice Cliff pottery was issued under her name (even though she worked for Wilkinsons) and the vast majority has a backstamp on the under-

Left to Right: Clarice Cliff Blue W Meiping Vase, 8.25 inches high, $3000. Orange Trees and House Shape 366 Vase, $1600. A pair of Shape 378 Vases in Oranges, $1200 each. Tennis Conical Jug, 6.5 inches high, $2200. *Photograph by and Courtesy of Bonhams, London UK/Bridgeman Art Library*

side declaring its pedigree. Similar backstamps were used for pottery produced by Susie Cooper and Charlotte Rhead.

As mentioned in the previous chapter, one of the greatest influences and factors in the success of Art Deco was the marriage with Industry. However, the later designs of British Art Deco ceramics were not subservient to industrial requirements. Indeed, the converse is probably true and the avant-garde shape designs no doubt stretched the previously traditional British Pottery industry to new found limits.

One aspect of Art Deco ceramics that is perverse to the industrial theme is that, to achieve the intensity and vigour of the patterns, it was necessary for them to be applied by hand painting. Thus, their production gave new light to craftsmanship.

Most of the British Art Deco ceramics were produced in earthenware. However, the major range from the Shelley Potteries was produced in very fine bone china and included some of the most stylish shapes available from any country in the Art Deco era.

Top row: Clarice Cliff Lotus Jug in the Secrets pattern, $2000. Isis Vase in the very rare May Avenue pattern, $9000. Lotus Jug in the Blue W pattern, $9000. Bottom row: Shape 187 Vase in Orange House, $2000. A Clouvre Marigold Isis Vase, $1900. Athens Jug in Newlyn, the alternative colorway of Forest Glen, $1100. Shape 342 Vase in Inspiration Aster, $1800. Shape 187 Vase in Green Autumn, $1800. *Photograph by and Courtesy of Bonhams. London UK/Bridgeman Art Library*

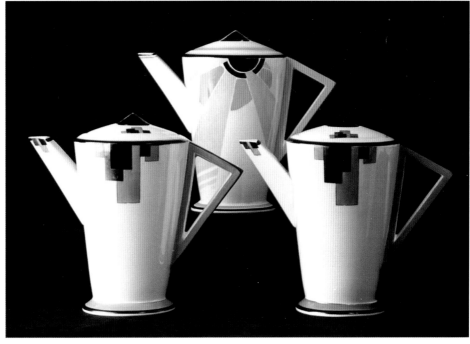

Three Shelley Vogue Coffeepots. *Courtesy of Decodance.* $400-550 each.

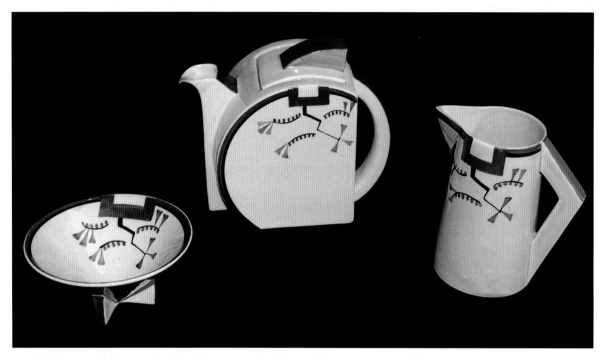

Stamford Teapot with Conical Milk and Sugar Bowl in the Ravel pattern. In 1948, the establishment, through the Council of Industrial Design, attempted to undermine the designs of Clarice Cliff, by circulating to colleges a picture of the conical jug with the caption, "Now fortunately outmoded but still to be seen, and avoided. The unfunctional handle and the decoration provide a useful cautionary study." *Courtesy of David Smith*. $1500 for the three.

One drawback suffered by the British potters was that, initially, the pottery upon which they added their decorations was of very traditional shapes. Consequently, the Original Bizarre designs of Clarice Cliff and the geometric designs of Susie Cooper are generally only available on less than ideal shapes. After her initial success, Clarice Cliff was allowed to introduce her own shapes. Susie Cooper had to leave her employment with Grays and open her own pottery to enable her to introduce more innovative shapes.

The end of the Art Deco era in the potteries was brought about by the second world war. The restrictions imposed against hand-painting for the home market, together with a change in mood and priorities of the British people, meant that the style would not survive. Just as the ending of the first world war had heralded a desire for a more colorful and stylish way of life, the start of World War Two demanded a return to austerity.

In Graham McLarens book, *Ceramics of the 1950s*, he suggests that the demise of Art Deco in the Potteries is rather more sinister. He points out that even the hand-painted wares for export were encouraged by the British government to be based on traditional floral and figural decorations in an attempt to "send subtle messages to the American people about the worth of the country they were helping to defend." Certainly, the designs of Clarice Cliff exports at this time (Tonquin and Orphelia, etc.), bear out this proposition. He also points out that after the end of the second world war, British government advisors attempted to impose their own designs on the pottery companies. These were based on plain functional utility pottery in an effort, according to Graham McLaren, "to banish the colorful legacy of Art Deco".[2] The British pottery industry, and the British people, vigorously rejected the idea of such utilitilitarian pottery. However, this led to a diluted Art Deco style in the years that followed the end of world war two.

Chapter 3
COLLECTING ART DECO CERAMICS

Top row: Clarice Cliff, The rear view of a Shape 464 Vase in Honolulu, a Shape 452 Stamford Vase in Honolulu, Lotus Jug, 11.5 inches in Honolulu, a Shape 358 Vase in Rudyard. Bottom row: a Rudyard pattern Conical Candlestick, Shape 384, 2 inches high, a Rudyard Daffodil Vase, Shape 450, a Shape 451 Vase in Rudyard. *Photograph by and Courtesy of Bonhams, London UK/ Bridgeman Art Library.* $1200-4000+.

THE GROWTH OF ART DECO COLLECTING

Art Deco is one of the growth areas in the antique/collectibles market. It enjoys not only a presence at general antique fairs, but it also has its own dedicated fairs in many parts of the world. In Britain, there is generally an Art Deco fair every other week of the year. All of the major auction houses around the world have regular Art Deco auctions (sometimes called Decorative Arts sales or Twentieth Century sales). The most popular sales held by Christies of London are their twice yearly sales exclusively of Clarice Cliff pottery.

There are many reasons for the popularity of Art Deco collecting. Art deco is still very much a feature of today's designs and, therefore, period pieces still have a very modern look. Consequently, they provide an easy fit with todays furnishings. Even though there may not be many people surviving today who actually lived in the era, many of us will recall seeing deco items in relatives houses and we may even have inherited such pieces. Art Deco provides a link to the past.

The spectrum of Art Deco collecting is extremely wide. However, by far the most popular items to collect are ceramics, and the most popular of those ceramics are British. British Art Deco ceramics are generally plentiful and widely available in all price ranges. Even a good example of Clarice Cliff pottery (the most famous of all Art Deco ceramic designers) can be obtained for as little as $350. This may, initially, seem a lot of money to pay for something like a plate. Although, in the great scheme of things in the antique world, it is a minor amount for a work of art.

STARTING A COLLECTION

Most people will start collecting with a "shotgun approach." They will acquire various items that appeal to them for different reasons, e.g. they may like a particular pattern or shape. Or it may be that a piece will fill a particular vacant spot in their home. They could also have possibly inherited some pottery.

After a few purchases, a theme will probably emerge. There is nothing wrong with the shotgun approach, as it gives you the opportunity to find your feet. However, do take stock of your initial collection as soon as you can, or else you may find that you very soon have a rather incongruous collection.

There are many themes for a collection. You could collect a selection of trios (cup/saucer/ plate) from the various potters. However, most people end up collecting examples from one or two specific designers. Unfortunately, even when you have decided which designers appeal to you, further refinement will be required. If, for example, you decide to collect Clarice Cliff, her range is so vast that, unless you specifically want a broad section collection, you will have to narrow it down to particular patterns and/or shapes. Some of the most dramatic collections I have seen have been centred on groupings of the same pattern on different shapes or different patterns on the same shape. Finally, as an alternative to a pattern or shape collection, you could concentrate on particular types of patterns, e.g. geometric, landscapes or stylized flowers.

A word of warning is needed. Collecting can be very addictive! You will find that, in a short period of time, your collection will have grown substantially. Whereas the initial problem may have been money, you will soon find that the major problem is space. Unless, you are fortunate to live in a large home, you need to be aware of this.

Many people strive to collect full tea or coffee sets and find that very soon they have no display areas left. I would suggest that if you do wish to collect sets, then you should limit yourself to only two cups and saucers. This will allow you to display a greater number of sets and it still looks very effective. Indeed, many original sets were only supplied with two cups and saucers and are known as Early Morning Sets.

I would also suggest that, once you have established a theme for your collection, you should, instead of buying three or four examples, wait and buy one more expensive special item. It may take you a while longer for you to feel that you have acquired a collection; however, ending up with a collection of special things is something that you will not regret. Too many times, have I seen collections where people have started buying rather mundane, cheaper items and have become locked into buying further similar items. They invariably regret their actions when they realise that they could have had, for the same financial outlay, a collection—albeit with less examples—that is far from mundane.

A further solution to the question of space is to collect small items. This is why such things as jampots, coffee cans, and conical sugar shakers are very popular with collectors. Unfortunately, however, due to their popularity, they are generally sold at a premium.

Kestrel shape Coffeepots by Susie Cooper in various colorways of the Graduating Black Bands pattern. *Courtesy of Decodance.* $250+ each.

A selection of Clarice Cliff Jam Pots in the Bonjour shape. Top Row: Delicia Pansies and Rodanthe. Bottom Row: Aurea, Xavier, Crocus and Coral Firs. $575-850.

BUYING

In addition to price, there are always three things to consider when buying— shape, pattern and condition. Many Art Deco designs were produced on both traditional and avant-garde shapes. Generally, the more avant-garde the shape, the more expensive it will be. Hence, a conical cup with a solid triangular handle will be far more expensive than a round cup with an open handle. A square stepped bowl will be far more expensive than a traditional round bowl. Although, with some patterns, you will not have the choice of shape, as they were limited to particular shapes. Generally, the earlier the piece, the more likely that it will be limited to a traditional shape, as many of the British factories used Art Deco as an opportunity to clear their backlogs of old shapes.

The pattern on a shape can also have a dramatic effect on the price. A Clarice Cliff bowl with the May Avenue pattern would probably sell for twenty times the price of the same shaped bowl with the Crocus pattern. Some patterns were also available in different color options, e.g. the Clarice Cliff pattern of Autumn was available in red, green, orange, blue and pastel. These are known as "colorways" and can have an effect on the price.

Certain patterns were not applied to the whole of the item, e.g. the pattern may be only painted on the edge of a plate and these are known as "shoulder patterns." Obviously, an item decorated in such a way will be far cheaper than one that features an all over pattern.

Even the same pattern can vary in price. As the majority of British Art Deco ceramics were hand painted by different individuals, you very often find that there may be a variance in the pattern, e.g. a particular landscape pattern may lack the usual cottage, reducing the value.

Whereas pattern and shape are somewhat subjective, the question of condition is rather more problematic. A lot of British Art Deco ceramics were made to be used, and consequently many examples surviving today are damaged. Damage can take the form of loss of paint to the pattern, chips, hairline cracks, scratching, and missing parts. Any damage to a piece will have an effect on price.

Damage to look out for includes chips to spouts and inner rims of teapots, chips to the outside edges of plates and saucers, and hairline cracks to vases or cup handles. When handling a plate, rub your finger around the edge of the plate. It is surprising how many chips you can discover that are not evident from a visual inspection. Also, ask yourself whether or not the piece should have a lid. This is particularly relevant to jampots, all of which generally came with a lid. I fear that many people have purchased jampots without lids, thinking they were acquiring a small vase or container. The usual giveaway is whether or not the piece has an inner rim at the top. You should also ask yourself whether or not the lid is the right one. Sometimes this is easier said than done. Many jampots were originally issued with lids having colored banding and not having the same pattern as the body of the piece itself. Generally, the banding on the lid should match the banding elsewhere on the piece. This is not always obvious and you can only rely on your research, instincts, and the honesty of the dealer.

Ideally, you should attempt to acquire undamaged pieces. You will, however, invariably have to accept less than perfect examples of hard to find objects as you become more specialised; otherwise, you may never acquire that missing item from your collection. It must also be accepted that very few examples will be in perfect condition and we have to accept an element of wear. As the majority of British Art Deco ceramics have the pattern hand painted on top of the glaze, it is inevitable that there will be a certain amount of paint loss. Bowls pose a particular problem. Many bowls were intended to hold fruit and the acid from the fruit may have adversely reacted with the inner decoration. The vast majority of pieces will also have traces of crazing. This cracking of the rigid glaze in thin lines across the surface of the pottery is caused by many years of contraction of the ceramic body beneath it through extreme changes in temperature. Most people in the deco era did not have the benefit of steady, controlled temperatures in their homes and their pottery was subjected to high temperatures during the daytime that plummeted at night. There are, of course, differing degrees of crazing. A piece can be so crazed that it is unacceptable. On the other hand, I would say that a piece without any signs of crazing could be suspect.

You will also have to consider the acceptability of restoration. If you buy a piece that is damaged, should you have it restored? This will depend, somewhat, on the value of the piece. It may not be economically viable to have it restored (unless it has some sentimental value). Some purists would argue that restoration is sac-religious. My own view is that, if it is financially viable, you should have it restored

properly as opposed to living with an annoying chip or hairline.

When buying, you should always try to detect any restoration. Even if it has been professionally done, it will have an effect on the price/value. Sometimes, restoration will be obvious. At other times, it may be impossible to detect. Things to look out for are changes in the colors of the pattern and any slightly uneven surface. Many of the paints used in the deco era contained lead and are no longer available. This means that some of the original colors can not be easily duplicated. To spot restored chips or hairlines in cups and bowls, place the item on the palm of one hand and tap it with a finger nail of the other hand. If the piece gives a clear ring, then it is probably fine. If it gives a thud, then it has possibly been restored.

If you wish to avoid pieces with restoration, do not want to worry over whether or not a piece has the right lid, and so on, the best advice is to buy from a reputable dealer. You will find that the majority of people dealing in Art Deco are enthusiasts themselves and rely on a good reputation. Buying at auction is a problem. The philosophy of most auction houses is "buyer beware" and you should, therefore, closely inspect items, before you bid on them.

Two Racing Car Teapots by James Sadler together with a Galleon by Burleigh Ware. *Photograph Courtesy of Bona Arts Decorative Ltd*. NP

Left: Clarice Cliff, an Early Morning Stamford Set in Honolulu, $6000+. Middle: a Stamford Teapot in Crocus, $1200. Right: an Early Morning Stamford Set in Pastel Autumn, $4500+. *Photograph by and Courtesy of Bonhams, London, UK/Bridgeman Art Library*

WHERE TO BUY

Probably, the most convenient way to buy is from an Art Deco dealer; either in a shop, mall, or at an antique fair. Try and visit an antique fair that is specifically for Art Deco or Twentieth Century items. Such events will give you the widest choice. In Britain, Art Deco fairs are held in all parts of the country. One of the largest Art Deco fairs in Europe is held at Battersea Town Hall in London on a regular basis. In the USA, you will probably have to travel to New York, Chicago, Miami, San Francisco or other major metropolitan areas.

As well as being businessmen/women, most Art Deco dealers are also collectors and enthusiasts. My experience is that they will gladly share their knowledge with anyone showing an interest in the subject.

As previously stated, it is also possible to buy pieces at auction. Many of the major auction houses hold special Art Deco sales and even if you do not buy from them, their catalogues are worth acquiring, as they are indispensable works of reference.

Buying at auction is, however, rather time consuming. In view of my previous comments relating to condition, you should, if possible, inspect the items on the viewing days. You will then have to return to bid on the item and may find that, after all that effort, you do not actually manage to buy anything. You can leave "commission bids" with the auction house to save you attending on the day. Although, if you successfully acquire an item through a commission bid, you will then have to arrange collection.

An alternative method of buying, that is rapidly finding favour, is to buy via the Internet. This can either be in the form of bidding in online auctions (which are generally held over seven day periods) or by viewing the stock of a dealer from his/ her web site and ordering by E-mail. This is certainly a convenient way to shop. Although, as in the case of conventional buying, you should attempt to establish a relationship with the dealer and appreciate that a reputable dealer is still a key ingredient for success.

FAKES AND REPRODUCTIONS

Criminals produce fakes to deceive. Unfortunately, the world of British Art Deco ceramics has not escaped the curse. Fakes are to be found among items purporting to be by Clarice Cliff, Carlton Ware, and Susie Cooper.

Clarice Cliff fakes take many forms, from out and out fakes to the despicable practice of painting valuable patterns on actual plain Clarice Cliff dinnerware. Carlton Ware has been particularly vulnerable in recent years. Stories abound regarding the theft of the old moulds to produce masses of unauthentic wares. Susie Cooper has generally escaped, except for a miniature Kestrel coffee set attributed to her in floral patterns that looks like something out of a doll's house. Susie Cooper never produced such things and I have seen them for sale at astronomical prices.

Once experienced, you should however not be overly troubled with fakes. Try to handle the real thing as much as possible and you should soon be able to spot most fakes. Fakes are generally badly painted, the colors do not look right, or the piece just looks too new. It has to be said, however, that there are fakes out there that will fool even the most experienced of collectors. Your insurance is to buy from a reputable dealer who will, even if duped himself, always refund your money if something turns out to be a fake. The vast majority of auction houses will also give you a refund.

Reproductions are different from fakes in that they do not, on the face of it, set out to deceive. They replicate the original and should be clearly marked (generally underneath) with a backstamp declaring their pedigree. The firm of Moorland manufactures a range of pottery that is based on Clarice Cliff patterns and shapes. All of these are clearly marked as reproductions and are made to sell at modest sums. Other reproductions are issued by the British pottery firm of Wedgwood, who owns the copyright of Clarice Cliff and Susie Cooper patterns and designs. These are usually issued in true limited editions and, like the originals, are hand painted.

Wedgwood, through the advice of the Clarice Cliff Collector's Club, generally choose to issue pieces based on the more expensive shapes and patterns of Clarice Cliff. Consequently, many collectors use the pieces to supplement their collections. Some purist collectors dismiss the idea of any reproductions. Still, the Wedgwood pieces are regarded as the best available and are frequently included in the sales of leading auction houses.

Notwithstanding the legitimacy of reproductions, there is a practice amongst some dealers and auction houses to offer them for sale (particularly the Moorland pieces) at vastly inflated prices. Presumably they hope that some unsuspecting new collector will think that they are buying the real thing.

PRICES

Constant advice is given to collectors only to buy pieces which they like and not to buy for investment. I agree that you should only buy pieces you like. However, I think it is unrealistic to ask collectors to ignore investment. You may not wish to dispose of your whole collection in the near future, but it is very likely that you may want to rationalise your collection and sell one or two pieces.

British Art Deco ceramics prices, particularly for Clarice Cliff, Carlton Ware and Shelley, have continued to rise over the last two decades. This trend, undoubtedly, has given confidence to the market. There is no evidence to suggest that prices will not continue to increase. Indeed, when you compare the prices of Art Deco antiques to other antiques, it is clear that prices have a long way to go. There is however, a general feeling in the deco trade that deco items are becoming harder to find and this could lead to a substantial increase in prices in the very near future.

Unlike most other goods, there is, of course, no fixed price for antiques and there is no new price to limit or determine second hand value. The only commercial factors are supply and demand and, perhaps, the necessity of dealers to maintain cash flows. Dealers' prices will be influenced by how much they paid for an item, the extent of their knowledge, and their overheads. Prices will therefore fluctuate between dealers and it is my experience that the more general dealers will over price the very mundane pieces of Clarice Cliff and sometimes under price the more valuable pieces. Although, at specialist Art Deco fairs, where competition is keen and dealers are somewhat more knowledgeable, there will generally be a "going rate" for some items. For example, a Clarice Cliff trio (cup/saucer/plate) in Crocus on a traditional shape will have a fairly standardised price of $225.

You should, however, treat isolated auction house prices with great caution. Just because an item has sold at one auction for a certain price, there is no guarantee that it will achieve the same result at another auction. Quite spectacular results have been recorded at auction when two individuals have become locked into a bidding battle. Also, to some people, money is no object. On more than one occasion I have sat next to someone who has flown in to attend a specialised Clarice Cliff auction with the intention of buying particular pieces, irrespective of cost.

Prices will also vary according to the country and the area of the country of purchase. Although, with the increasing familiarity with and popularity of the Internet, the world is becoming a much smaller market place and prices are becoming globalized.

SUSIE COOPER

Chapter 4

Susie Cooper, photographed by Cleo Cotterell in 1938.
*By kind permission of Ellesborough Ltd., Isle of Man.
Photograph courtesy of Josiah Wedgwood & Sons Ltd.*

Susie Cooper was a woman of haunting beauty. Her career as a pottery designer spanned over seventy years, and she was responsible for over 4500 patterns. She staggered the pottery industry by establishing her own pottery in a male dominated industry. Her success was achieved through her artistic and innovative talents combined with hard work and determination. Many honours have been bestowed on her. The Royal Society of Arts awarded her the "Royal Designer for Industry" award in 1940. At the time, Susie was both the first business woman and the youngest person to receive the award. Later, in 1979, she was awarded the Order of the British Empire by the Queen. At the award ceremony, the Queen Mother revealed that she was still using Susie Cooper pottery.

Susan Vera Cooper, was born on the 29th October 1902 at Burslem, in The Potteries. From a very early age she was known by all as Susie. Her family was middle-class and had many business interests in the area.

She attended the Burslem School of Art, where she was taught by Gordon Forsyth. There she excelled in wood carving, painting, and clay modeling. Whilst at the art school, she applied for a scholarship to attend the Royal College of Art to study fashion design. Her application was rejected on the grounds that applicants had to be already working in an industry associated with Decorative Arts. Consequently, to satisfy the requirement, Gordon Forsyth advised her to take up employment with the pottery firm of A.E.Gray & Co. Ltd. for a short period to gain the scholarship. For a young girl from a middle-class background, this was, on the face of it, not an appropriate position.

Susie Cooper, started work for Grays in 1922. She was under the impression that she would be employed as a designer. However, to her distress, that post had already been filled by another young lady. Susie Cooper, therefore, commenced work as a paintress. She was, however, very quickly promoted to a designer at the factory when the other young lady, a Miss Samuels, failed to return after a holiday.[1]

The first recorded reference to Susie Cooper's pottery is the inclusion of some of her designs in the catalogue for an exhibition called "British institute of industrial art, recent examples of British pottery," held at the Victoria and Albert museum in London in 1923.[2]

Her first designs, in conjunction with Gordon Forsyth, were a range of lustre wares. Some of these items were exhibited at the 1925 Paris exhibition and won a silver medal, although the pattern that won the medal is not known.

Problems were, however, encountered with the lustre wares. The thin layer of decoration

Left: The Susie Cooper Pottery Float at the annual "Crazy Day" Carnival, Stoke on Trent, early 1930s. *Photograph courtesy of the Trustees of The Wedgwood Museum, Barleston, Staffordshire, England.*

Below: A promotional photograph of 1933, featuring many of the Studio wares being produced by the Susie Cooper Pottery. *Photograph courtesy of the Trustees of The Wedgwood Museum, Barleston, Staffordshire, England.*

was susceptible to wear and was not very practicable for tableware.

Susie Cooper then moved on to produce on glaze boldly painted floral designs, utilizing freehand brushwork. At this time, Grays created a special backstamp for the Susie Cooper designs. The new backstamp continued the firm's theme of ships; but, instead of the traditional galleons used in the past, the new backstamp depicted a modern ocean liner. Together with the backstamp, each piece of pottery included the wording "designed by Susie Cooper," creating a designer label image.

The first geometric Susie Cooper patterns were released in 1928. They were extremely abstract designs heavily influenced by De Stijl and Cubism. The Pottery Gazette, in 1929, reported on one of the coffee sets as being "...somewhat cubist in type, with blobs of color and streaks, with the blues, greens and reds violently contrasted."

The geometric patterns were executed with very thick brush strokes and actually used the imprint of the strokes to make up the patterns. Unlike Clarice Cliff pottery, outlining was not used, and the colors were painted freehand. These geometrics, in design terms, were the closest that Susie Cooper came to Clarice Cliff.

Being thickly painted on glaze, the patterns were susceptible to flaking and scratching. As experienced by Clarice Cliff, the blue enamel posed a particular problem. Consequently, many examples found today, show distinct wear and blue paint loss. Due to the lack of durability, Susie Cooper somewhat rejected these designs. Ironically, however, her geometric patterns are the most collectible of all Susie Cooper designs and demand the highest prices.

Most of the geometric patterns that Susie Cooper produced for Grays are inevitably found on traditional shapes. One reason for this is that Grays did not manufacture their own shapes; instead, they bought them in and acted as a decorating enterprise. However, the complete over-painting of the body of the pottery, together with the boldness of the patterns, completely overtakes the shape and makes it somewhat irrelevant. Susie Cooper's geometrics possess a great sense of immediacy and the strident designs can be a shock to the uninitiated.

Designed by Susie Cooper for Grays. Various items shown in the Moon and Mountains pattern, c. 1928. Pattern No. 7960. Coffee Can and Saucer, $300; Sugar Bowl, $225; small Coaster, $175; Milk Jug, $225. *Courtesy of Decodance.*

Bowl in Moon &
Mountains pattern.
*Photograph by and
courtesy of Keiko
Okabe*. $600.

Cup and Saucer
Moon and
Mountains.
*Photograph by and
courtesy of Keiko
Okabe*. $220.

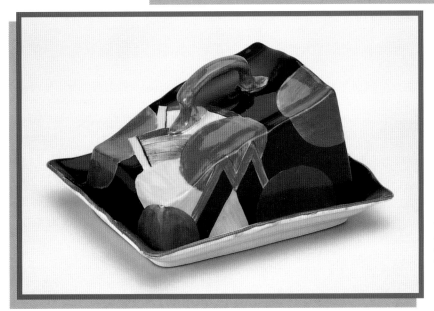

Butterdish in In Moon
and Mountains.
*Photograph by and
courtesy of Keiko
Okabe*. $450.

Many of the geometric patterns of this time do not have official names and have been given suitable names by collectors over the years. One of the first patterns in the strident geometric style is pattern number 7960, which is better known to collectors as Moon and Mountains. This is probably the best known of all the Susie Cooper geometrics. As the name suggests, it features full moonlike colored circles with geometric triangles standing proudly to the front.

In 1929, the Cubist pattern (one of the few geometric patterns to be actually named by Susie Cooper) followed. Like Moon and Mountains, this was also very successful and was applied to coffee sets, tea sets, vases, jugs and

Paris Jug by Susie Cooper for Grays in the Moon and Mountains pattern. Pattern No. 7960. *Courtesy of Decodance.* $450.

Tea for Two in the Cubist pattern. *Photograph by and courtesy of Keiko Okabe.* $1500.

Advertising Jug for Ross's Grapefruit Drink in the Cubist pattern. *Photograph by and courtesy of Keiko Okabe.* $450.

cigarette boxes. It was also featured on a range of advertising wares for Ross tonic water and grapefruit drinks, that included water jugs and ashtrays. Other geometric patterns featured chevrons, arced spikes and overlapping triangles.

Whilst at Grays, Susie Cooper experimented with banding and many of her patterns were made up exclusively of banding. Whereas Grays did not design their own shapes, Susie Cooper did manage to design a few shapes for Grays. These included a coffee pot and a jug. Frustrated, by her lack of opportunity to design shapes, and constantly annoyed by the companies sales force dictating what they thought would sell, she left her employment with Grays in October 1929.

Inverted Bowl for
Grays in the
Cubist pattern.
*Photograph by and
courtesy of Keiko
Okabe.* $450.

Graduated Jugs by
Susie Cooper for Grays
in the Cubist pattern.
*Courtesy of
Decodance.* $275-500.

A Lemonade Jug by
Susie Cooper for Grays
in the Cubist pattern.
Courtesy of Decodance.
$700.

Coffee Cans by Susie Cooper in Pattern No. 8117. *Photograph by and courtesy of Keiko Okabe.* $200 each.

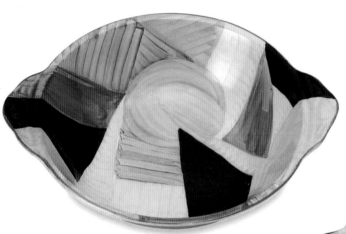

Handled Bowl in Pattern No. 8078. *Photograph by and courtesy of Keiko Okabe.* $350.

Two Handled Bowl with chevron and geometric pattern. Pattern No. 8828. *Photograph by and courtesy of Keiko Okabe.* $350.

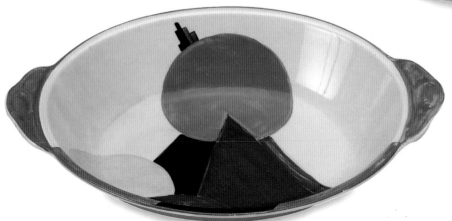

Unusual pattern on a Two Handled Bowl for Grays. *Photograph by and courtesy of Keiko Okabe.* $350.

Above: Part Coffee Set in Pattern No. 8212. Liner mark for Grays. The shape of the Coffeepot was also designed by Susie Cooper. *Photograph by and courtesy of Keiko Okabe.* $1800.

Left: A Susie Cooper Bowl in Patten No. 8212. *Courtesy of Decodance.* $500.

Below: Bowl by Susie Cooper for Grays. Painted with Pattern No. 8212, 8 inch diameter. *Courtesy of Decodance.* $500.

Top: Paris Jug in Pattern No. 8078. Susie Cooper Liner mark for Grays. *Photograph by and courtesy of Keiko Okabe*. $350.

Center: Paris Jug for Grays in overlapping swirling lines. Susie Cooper Liner mark. *Photograph by and courtesy of Keiko Okabe*. $350.

Bottom: Paris Jug for Grays. *Photograph by and courtesy of Keiko Okabe*. $300.

Sugar Bowl by Susie Cooper for Grays in the Overlapping Triangles pattern, c. 1929. Pattern No. 8127. *Courtesy of Decodance*. $225.

Above: Triangular Planter in Overlapping Triangles pattern. Pattern No. 8127. *Photograph by and courtesy of Keiko Okabe.* $450.

Right: Paris Jug by Susie Cooper for Grays in the Overlapping Triangles pattern. Pattern No. 8127. *Courtesy of Decodance.* $250.

Octagonal Bowl by Susie Cooper for Grays in Pattern No. 8078, 7 inch diameter. *Courtesy of Decodance.* $400.

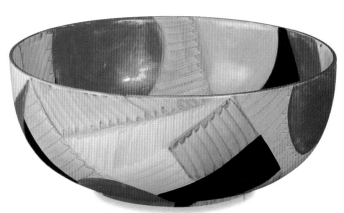

Bowl by Susie Cooper for Grays. Internally and externally decorated with Pattern No. 8078, 8 inch diameter. *Courtesy of Decodance.* $500.

A Grays part Coffee Set in Pattern No. 8872. The Coffeepot was one of the few shapes Susie Cooper designed for Grays. *Courtesy of Decodance.* $1100.

A 10 inch Plate in Pattern No. 8078. *Courtesy of Decodance.* $600.

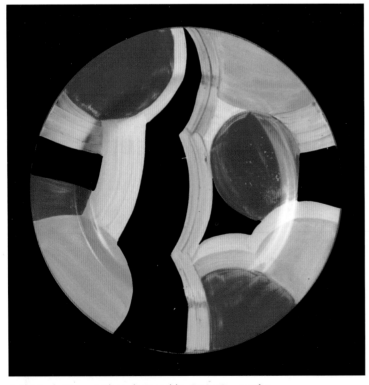

A 6.5 inch Dessert Plate designed by Susie Cooper for Grays Pattern No. 8212. *Courtesy of Decodance.* $250.

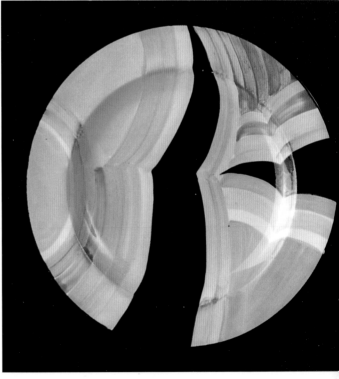

A 6.5 inch Dessert Plate in Pattern No. 8117. Susie Cooper Liner mark for Grays. *Courtesy of Decodance.* $250.

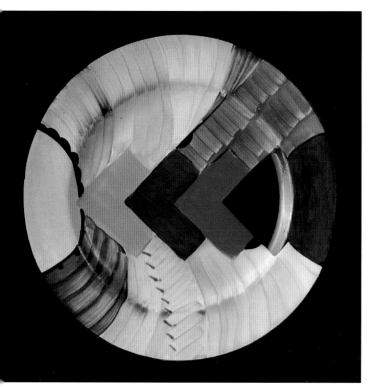

One of the first Geometric designs by Susie Cooper for Grays was the Cubist pattern shown here on a 7 inch Dessert Plate. *Courtesy of Decodance.* $250.

A 6.25 inch Plate by Susie Cooper in the Moon and Mountains pattern. Liner mark for Grays, Pattern No. 7960. *Courtesy of Decodance.* $250.

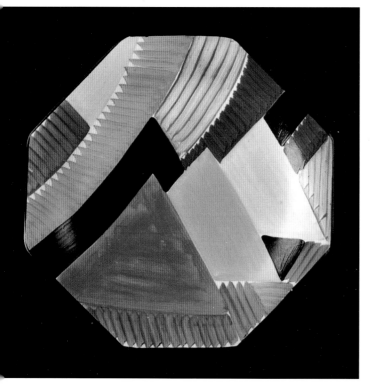

A small Plate from a Sandwich Set in the Overlapping Triangles pattern, Pattern No. 8127. *Courtesy of Decodance.* $220.

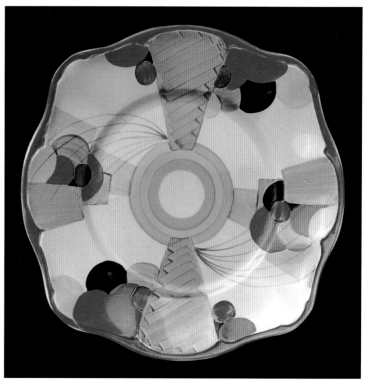

Grays Plate, pattern unknown. *Courtesy of Decodance.* $200.

With financial backing from her family, Susie took the bold step of opening her own pottery firm. She set up premises at the George Street Pottery in Tunstall, together with six paintresses. The location was ill fated, due to the financial difficulties of her landlord. New premises were hurriedly found at the Chelsea Works in Burslem. Pottery production started there in 1930. The catch phrase used by the firm in advertising was "elegance with utility." Apparently, the pottery industry and Gordon Forsyth were rather taken aback by the thought of a woman starting such a business venture.

Success, soon followed and orders were later received from Harrods and Selfridges. Patterns were issued utilising stylized flowers together with the continued use of geometrics. The geometric patterns, however, took on a different form. They became more subdued, sophisticated, and not quite so "in your face" as the earlier Grays patterns. Due to a reduction of the painted areas, they were quicker to produce and overcame the flaking problem.

The demand for Susie Cooper pottery led her to move the company, in 1931, to new premises at The Crown Works in Burslem. By this time, the workforce had been greatly expanded. It was here that Susie Cooper introduced her famous Leaping Deer backstamp.[3] Given her new found independence, one of the first of her new shapes was a redesign of a tankard made by the pottery firm of Wood and Sons. To this basic shape she applied an innovative streamlined handle. She used the existing contours of the body to contain banded decoration.[4]

Her first major shape design to have a long lasting effect, however, was the Kestrel shape. This shape was exhibited at the 1932 British Industries Fair and the range included milk jugs, cups and teapots. The most dramatic piece in the range, however, was the Kestrel coffee pot.

The Kestrel coffee pot is a masterpiece of design. It combines well with any type of deco-

Lemonade Set for Grays. *Photograph by and courtesy of Keiko Okabe*. $900.

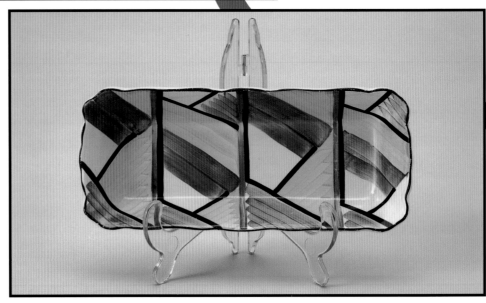

Sandwich Tray. *Photograph by and courtesy of Keiko Okabe*. $300.

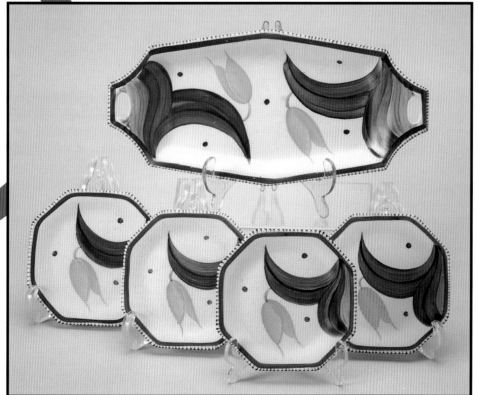

Above: A Susie Cooper Tea for Two, in the Cube shape, with the very rare Panorama pattern. Pattern No. E/306. Black Triangle backstamp. *Courtesy of Banana Dance.* $2000+.

Left: Sandwich Set in Tulips Pattern, Pattern No. E61, c. 1930. One of the first patterns produced by Susie Cooper after she established her own pottery firm. *Photograph by and courtesy of Keiko Okabe.* $1100.

Above: Coffee Can and Saucer in Pattern No. E279. *Photograph by and courtesy of Keiko Okabe.* $180.

Right: Donegal Ashtray by Susie Cooper. *Courtesy of Alison Dobbs.* NP

Trio of items in Pattern No. E279 by Susie Cooper. *Courtesy of Alison Dobbs.* NP

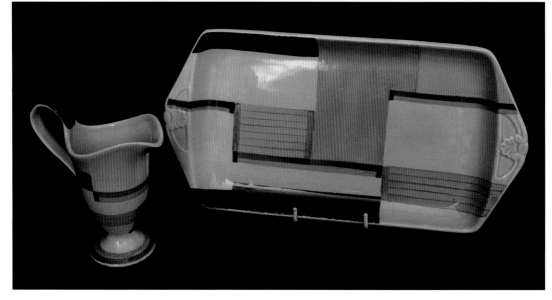

Sandwich Tray and Empire shape Milk Jug in Pattern No. E237. A later geometric pattern by Susie Cooper. *Courtesy of Alison Dobbs.* NP

ration, from traditional florals to polka dots to blocks of geometric colors. It seems to stand proud in any setting and declares itself a successful mix of sophistication and functionality. The roundness of the body and the handle make it inviting to touch. The body of the spout appears cranelike and the tip pouts like a bird. Even the lid, which locks into position, is topped with a crest to provide a streamlined effect.

The locking device of the lid, as innovative as it is—and it must have saved many a lid falling off when coffee was poured—does unfortunately present todays collectors with a slight drawback. In order to take the lid off, it must be first turned. This has obviously been a problem to users in the past, as many Kestrel examples have damaged inner rims, caused by people forcing the lid off improperly. Even today, at antique fairs, people can be seen struggling with this lid.

Notwithstanding such problems, practicality was always a pursuit of Susie Cooper. In 1933, a Kestrel tureen was registered with the patent office. The special feature of the design was that the lid, turned upside down, could act as a freestanding dish itself and was easily stacked. The tureen was exhibited at the British Industries Fair of 1933 and reports on the fair described it as an "ingenious invention."

A multitude of patterns were applied to the Kestrel range, including the very sophisticated Graduating Black Bands (a name given by the writer Andrew Casey).

Tankard by Susie Cooper. This was one of the first shapes designed by Susie Cooper after establishing the Crown Works. It was a reworking of a tankard by Wood & Sons and incorporated an innovative streamlined handle. *Courtesy of Decodance.* $180.

Above: Coffee Set by Susie Cooper in Blue Graduating Black Bands pattern. Marked with Leaping Deer backstamp and No. 501. *Courtesy of Decodance.* $1200+.

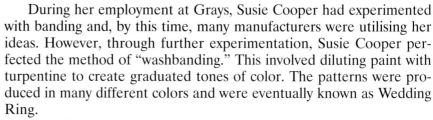

During her employment at Grays, Susie Cooper had experimented with banding and, by this time, many manufacturers were utilising her ideas. However, through further experimentation, Susie Cooper perfected the method of "washbanding." This involved diluting paint with turpentine to create graduated tones of color. The patterns were produced in many different colors and were eventually known as Wedding Ring.

By 1934, the demand for Susie Cooper pottery, both at home and abroad, was becoming insatiable. To meet the demand, Susie Cooper turned from hand-painting to lithographs and created Dresden Spray, which was to become one of her most famous patterns. In contrast to previous patterns, this was undoubtedly a traditional design, but was regarded at the time as being extremely technically innovative.

Other successful lithographs followed, including Patricia Rose and Swansea Spray. Nicholaus Pevsner, writing in "Trend in Design," stated, "I know of only a few cases where adventurous potters have begun to design modern lithographs to satisfy their standards. Miss Susie Cooper, so far as I know, was the first to do this."

Whereas her patterns of the latter part of the decade echoed a restrained naturalistic style, Susie Cooper went from strength to strength, supplying pottery to exclusive stores, airlines, and even the British Parliament.

Left: Kestrel Coffeepot in Tango Orange Graduating Black Bands. *Courtesy of Decodance.* $240.

Below: Coffee Set by Susie Cooper in Yellow Graduating Black Bands. *Courtesy of Decodance.* $900+ for the set.

Above: A further colorway of the Graduating Black Bands pattern. *Courtesy of Decodance.* $800+ for the set.

Below: Coffee Set by Susie Cooper in Orange Graduating Black Bands. *Courtesy of Decodance.* $900+ for the set.

Above: A Susie Cooper Kestrel Coffeepot in a washbanded pattern. Marked with Leaping Deer backstamp and No. 481. *Courtesy of Decodance.* $160.

Right: An extremely rare Wall Mask modelled and signed by Susie Cooper herself, 12 inches high. In the 1930s, Susie Cooper made four masks: Chinaman, Judge, Brunette (also known as Greta Garbo), and the one pictured (which is sometimes referred to as "Blonde"). They are all rare, but this is the rarest of the four as it was never put into commercial production. It is believed to be a self portrait of Susie Cooper and was hung in her studio and in her London Show-rooms from 1934-1939. The Mask is the current record holder for a price paid for a Susie Cooper piece. *Photograph by and Courtesy of Sotheby's.* $10000.

IDENTIFYING SUSIE COOPER

GRAYS

Generally, all Grays pottery bears a backstamp and the majority has a pattern number. The first Susie Cooper pattern for the company is thought to be pattern number 2866 (a simple floral design) and the last somewhere in the region of number 8600. Caution should, however, be exercised when attributing a pattern between these numbers, as it is thought that Grays employed other designers during the time that Susie Cooper worked for them. Indeed, on the assumption that pattern numbers run consecutively, it would have been a great feat for Susie Cooper to have designed over 6000 patterns in a period of seven years.

Adrian Woodhouse suggests that Susie Cooper patterns actually go beyond 8600 and extend well into the 8800s.[5] This is certainly supported by pattern number 8872, which shows the distinct Susie Cooper geometric style.

Backstamps can also help in dating Grays pottery and attributing designs to Susie Cooper. The usual backstamp applied to her designs is the Liner backstamp. Although, be aware that there are many examples of her designs in existence that bear either the Galleon or Clipper backstamps. It also appears that Susie Cooper designs continued to be issued by Grays long after she left the company.

Susie Cooper in later years, working at home on her "Black Fruit" designs. *Photograph courtesy of the Trustees of The Wedgwood Museum, Barleston, Staffordshire, England.*

POST-GRAYS

All the pottery produced by Susie Cooper in the deco era (with the exception of a handful of examples) was made of earthenware. Generally, any bone china items which you may encounter will at the earliest be from the 1950s.

The first independent backstamp used at the George Street premises was a triangle containing the words "A Susie Cooper production" and with "Tunstall" stamped below. The same backstamp was used at the Chelsea works, except underneath the triangle is the word "Burslem".

The move, in 1931, to the Crown works saw the introduction of the Leaping Deer backstamp. The Leaping Deer was used alongside numerous other backstamps, including those containing facsimile signatures.

Almost all Susie Cooper pottery will carry one of her backstamps. Notable exceptions, however, are the items she specifically made for the London stores of John Lewis and Peter Jones. These items, including the Kestrel shapes, feature the name of the store as the only mark, with or without the pattern name. A fairly frequent example found today is the Kestrel coffee pot in the Polka Dot pattern.

Pattern numbers for independent Susie Cooper pottery start at number E/50 and run consecutively up to approximately 1824 for the year 1940. The numbers started at 50 to conceal the newness of the company. Frequently, the pattern number and sometimes the name of the pattern, will be marked on the bottom of the piece. And, in some cases,

the number will be entered into a special box, forming part of the backstamp.

It should be remembered, however, that many patterns were in production for many years. Consequently, all a pattern number can tell us, in terms of age, is the year that the pattern was first introduced. Although, by reference to lists, they can identify a pattern.

Set out below are the approximate first pattern numbers for each year up to 1940.[6]

1929	50	1935	920
1930	100	1936	1121
1931	200	1937	1345
1932	356	1938	1417
1933	617	1939	1636
1934	700		

BACKSTAMPS

Grays. From c. 1931.

Grays. From c. 1923 to c. 1931.

Leaping Deer. From c. 1932 to c. 1964.

From c. 1932.

From c. 1933 to c. 1964.

44

Chapter 5

CLARICE CLIFF

The story of Clarice Cliff is a classic rags to riches fairytale. Unlike Charlotte Rhead, she was not born into a famous family and, unlike Susie Cooper, she was not to grow up in middle class comfort.

Clarice Cliff was born in January 1899 to working class parents. Her family home was a small terraced house at Tunstall, in The Potteries, where she lived with her mother, father, two brothers and five sisters. Her home surroundings and early life were very much the same as thousands of other children in the area. And like them, her inevitable destiny would be to work in the pottery industry. However, unlike the majority of pottery workers, who would merely scratch a living from their work, Clarice Cliff was to acquire fame and wealth that even she could not have imagined. She was to become a role model and the most famous of all Art Deco pottery designers, both during her lifetime and after.

At the age of 13, Clarice Cliff left school and went to work for Lingard Webster & Co. as an apprentice paintress. Three years later, in 1915, she moved to the pottery firm of Hollinshead and Kirkham to work as a lithographer. After one year with that firm, she left and went to work for the pottery firm of Wilkinsons, and this was to be a major milestone in her life.

Wilkinsons was quite a large pottery firm that was run and owned by a Mr. Colley Shorter. Her first job there was to apply transfers to pottery in the lithograph department and she did this work for a period of four years. In 1920, however, her enthusiasm and talents were partly recognised and she was moved to assist John Butler and Fred Ridgeway, who were two of the top designers at the factory. With them, she assisted in producing prestige pieces for the factory. Clarice was given the job of executing the gold outlining.[1]

In 1922, Clarice signed her apprenticeship Indentures with Wilkinsons as a Modeler. She also later attended a formal modelling course at The Burslem School of Art, under the direction of Gordon Forsyth, who was a major influence and shaper of the output of many of the potteries in the Deco era. As was usual with such courses, students were required to produce a final examination piece. A recent discovery of a figurine, signed by Clarice Cliff and dated 1925, suggests that this particular piece has now been found. Following consultation with Wedgwood, it has been decided to name the figurine "the Turquoise Ring."

It is obvious from the figurine that Clarice possessed great modelling skills. It also appears that she was allowed to produce various models at the Wilkinsons factory. She was very soon given her own private studio at the adjacent Newport factory (which Wilkinsons had previously purchased) and Colley Shorter was to be a frequent visitor.

From subsequent events, it appears that Colley's interest in Clarice went beyond their working relationship. Whereas, Clarice could not be described as a woman of beauty, she was a vivacious brunette with a flair for fashion. Colley was seventeen years older than Clarice, married, and had two children. In the 1920s, any such relationship between an upper class married man and a working class factory girl would have met with great distain. To further speculation about the relationship, Clarice did something highly unusual for the time. She moved out of her family home into a flat at the nearby town of Hanley. This caused a rift with her family and fuelled the rumours. It is quite possible that, given the situation, Cliff's friends and colleagues may have

Clarice Cliff. Courtesy of Len Griffin, Louis K. and Susan Pear Meisel, and Abrams/Thames

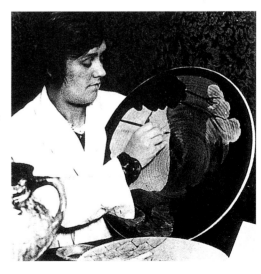

and Hudson.

treated her with an element of caution. The forced alienation may have driven Clarice to concentrate more on her work and aspirations. Whatever the feelings of the day, the relationship between Colley and Clarice, was to be a major factor in her success.

During her career, Clarice designed over 500 patterns and 750 shapes. Whereas she was influenced by other artists and even borrowed patterns and designs, she was a catalyst for the British pottery industry.

Her talents, combined with the marketing skills of Colley Shorter, projected her in her lifetime to a position of fame and wealth. Her pottery is now avidly collected by enthusiasts all over the world and she enjoys her true position as the world's most famous Art Deco pottery designer.

SELECTION OF CLARICE CLIFF SHAPES

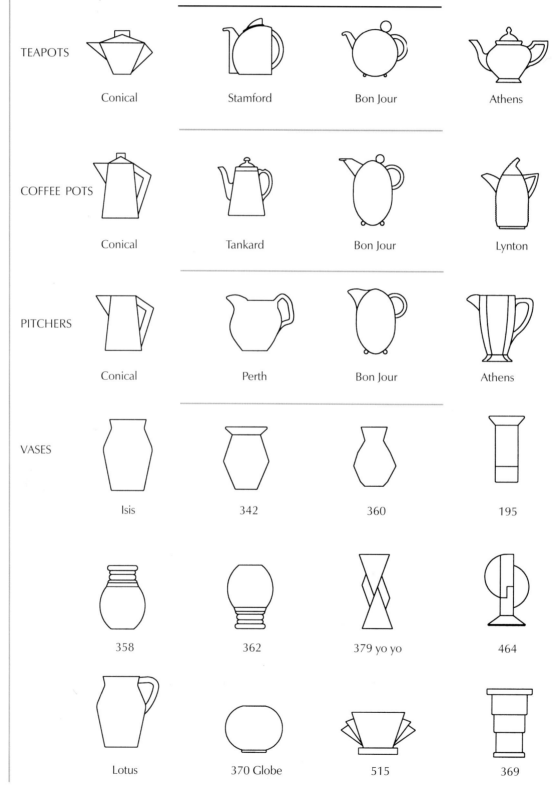

TEAPOTS

Conical   Stamford   Bon Jour   Athens

COFFEE POTS

Conical   Tankard   Bon Jour   Lynton

PITCHERS

Conical   Perth   Bon Jour   Athens

VASES

Isis   342   360   195

358   362   379 yo yo   464

Lotus   370 Globe   515   369

Illustrations by John Murray

ORIGINAL BIZARRE

In 1927, Clarice Cliff went to London for a two month course at The Royal College of Art in Kensington to study clay modelling. At that time, she also visited Paris, and during her visit she no doubt immersed herself in the culture of the French designers. Certainly, some of her designs that were to follow were heavily influenced by Cubism and Fauvism. It is also known that after her return from Paris, Clarice purchased folios of pochoir prints by Edouard Benedictus and Serge Gladky. These were to also influence some of her later designs.[2]

When Wilkinsons purchased the adjoining Newport factory, they also acquired vast stocks of undecorated pieces of pottery in old fashioned shapes, many of which had defects. Clarice suggested that she be allowed to decorate the pieces in bold colors, hiding the defects and revitalising them to make them salable. The idea struck a chord with Colley, and no doubt he saw a marketing opportunity for an otherwise redundant stock.

Originally, just one paintress, Gladys Scarlet, was assigned to the project. However, very soon, many more were to follow. Clarice instructed them to emphasise the hand-painting by using exaggerated brush strokes. The resultant designs covered the whole of the visible pottery body. These designs were simple geometrics based on triangles, generally outlined in brown, black or green. Shapes used by Clarice included the Globe teapot, Tankard coffee pot, Empire cups, and Lotus jugs and a multitude of vases that included the Meiping shape.

Top Row: A pair of Oranges and Lemons pattern Vases, Shape 451, 8 inches high, $1500 each. A pair of Sunburst pattern Vases, Shape 280, 6.25 inches high, $1200 each. A Cubist pattern Archaic series Vase, marked "Fantasque Republica Temple Luxor Thebes capital of the large columns 1250 BC", $3000. A Farmhouse pattern, bhape 451 Vase, $800. A Castellated Circle pattern, shape 279 Vase, $1200. Bottom row: Conical Bowl, Shape 382 with a Geometric pattern, $2000. An Orange Picasso Flower pattern Stamford Jardiniere. This was also sold with a lid as a Biscuit Barell, $850. Conical Bowl with geometric design, $1500. *Photograph by and Courtesy of Bonhams, London UK/Bridgeman Art Library*

Figurine by Clarice Cliff. Thought to be her Examination piece for her modelling course at The Burslem School of Art. *Photograph by and courtesy of Harold and Maureen.* NP

The base of the figurine, signed by Clarice Cliff herself and dated 1925.

Pochoir by Serge Gladky.

Colley Shorter received the designs with enthusiasm. He undertook a marketing plan that was to include hand-painting demonstrations by Clarice and others at major stores. A later promotional tool was the creation of the "Bizooka." This was a large horse-like figure made up of different examples of Clarice's pottery and was exhibited at various places. For the 1999 Centenary Exhibition of Clarice Cliff pottery, the Bizooka was recreated by Wedgwood and displayed at the Wedgwood Museum in Stoke on Trent.

The travelling salesman employed by Wilkinsons were given samples and were sent out on the road to convince shop buyers to purchase the range. The designs were immediately successful and their production was increased. At first the designs were marked just with the name Bizarre, hand painted on the underside of each piece.

The Pottery Gazette and Glass Trade Review of March 1928 reported that "a new range of wares ... has been styled Bizarre Ware, and if the name is intended to convey that the designs are singular and capricious, then it is thoroughly apt."

Later, however, in one of the most shrewd and effective marketing ploys ever, a backstamp was introduced declaring "Hand painted by Clarice Cliff." This established the Clarice Cliff "designer label" that became highly collectible in its own time and remains so today.

The early Clarice Cliff designs must have had a dramatic effect on the buying public. They were vivid and strident and were probably regarded by many as being shocking.

If any criticism can be leveled, then it is that some of the designs were, due to the circumstances of the project, only found on old fashioned shapes. On close analysis, these shapes are incongruous with the designs. Yet, the combination does fuel the concept of them being bizarre.

Bowl in Original Bizarre. *Courtesy of Decodance.* $350.

Above: Bowl in Original Bizarre, c. 1928. One of the very early pieces. Handpainted Red Bizarre mark. *Courtesy of Decodance.* $375.

Left: Bowl in Original Bizarre. *Courtesy of Decodance.* $320.

A Clarice Cliff Octagonal Plate in Original Bizarre. *Courtesy of Decodance.* $400.

An Ashtray in Original Bizarre, c. 1928.
Courtesy of Decodance. $300.

An Original Bizarre Trio with a traditionally shaped
Empire Cup. Marked Bizare with a gold backstamp.
Courtesy of Decodance. $500.

Above: A Fernpot in Original
Bizarre, height 3 inch, c.
1928. *Courtesy of Decodance.*
$480.

Left: Two Original Bizarre
Fernpots. *Courtesy of Banana
Dance.* $600+ each.

A selection of Lotus and Isis Jugs by Clarice Cliff. Top Row: Double V, Diamonds, Original Bizarre, Fruitburst and Windbells. Middle Row: Pastel Melon, Blue Chintz, House and Bridge, Inspiration Tulip, and Trees and House. Bottom Row: Original Bizarre, Inspiration Lily, Forest Glen, Caprice, and Autumn. *Photograph by and Courtesy of Carole A Berk Ltd.* $2500-9500 +.

THE BIZARRE RANGE

Contrary to what some people will tell you, and with the exception of Original Bizarre, Bizarre is not the name of a Clarice Cliff pattern. It is the name of a range of patterns introduced by Clarice Cliff from circa 1927 to 1936.

Bizarre covered a multitude of patterns including landscapes, traditional and stylized florals, and geometrics. The patterns were applied to every conceivable item of pottery from tableware to vases to ashtrays. To denote the introduction of the range, a special backstamp was created "Hand Painted Bizarre by Clarice Cliff".

The decoration of Bizarre Ware was carried out in a separate workshop at the factory, where up to sixty girls—known as the Bizarre Girls—were employed. The patterns were generally outlined by one section of girls, then passed to another section for the patterns to be painted in, and finally to the banders to add the colored banding to the top, bottom and rims of the pieces.

A special glaze, called Honeyglaze, was used on the majority of the Bizarre and Fantasque pieces. This glaze gives the pottery (and hence the background to the patterns) a warm glow.

In 1928, Clarice released the Crocus pattern. This, unlike the earlier geometrics, was a traditional type floral pattern. It was, however, to become her best seller and to be known as her "signature pattern." It was available on al-

The most popular pattern released by Clarice Cliff was Crocus. It was issued in various colorways and is seen here in the most popular Autumn Crocus. As shown, it was applied to every conceivable shape. *Photograph by and Courtesy of Carole A Berk Ltd.* $120-3500.

An Athens Jug in the Crocus pattern.
Courtesy of Decodance. $375.

Fernpot in Crocus. *Courtesy
of Decodance.* $280.

Various shapes shown decorated with the Autumn
Crocus pattern. *Courtesy of Decodance.* $175-600.

most every shape issued by the factory and sold well throughout her whole career. It was so successful that it was available in many different colorways and variations, including Peter Pan Crocus, Autumn Crocus, Spring Crocus, and Sungleam Crocus. To meet demand, a separate Crocus workshop, employing up to thirty paintresses, was established.

Also in 1928, the Ravel pattern was introduced. This was somewhat of a digression for Clarice. Ravel was a very restrained and minimalist geometric pattern. It must, however, have appealed to the buying public as it was produced in great quantities up to 1935.

Not content with designing patterns, Clarice turned her attention to new shapes. Some of the first shapes introduced by her were geometric vases (shape numbers 360, 365, 366, and 369), inspired by the French designer Robert Lallemant.[3]

Shortly after, Clarice pioneered further shapes based on a cone. This led to the Yo Yo vase, the Conical bowl, and Conical teaware, all shapes that are now regarded as quintessential Clarice Cliff Art Deco. Patterns introduced in 1929 to decorate the conical range were also greatly influenced by Art Deco. They included Sunray, Lightning, Football, Diamonds, Castellated Circle, Blue W and Double V. These patterns were a natural progression from Original Bizarre, but were much more sophisticated and complex.

Various patterns were introduced in 1930. Due to the success of Crocus, a further traditional floral, Gayday, was released. And continuing the cubist and abstract themes, the year also saw Carpet, Swirls, and Picasso Flower.

At this time, Clarice also took the bold step of experimenting with her Age of Jazz figures. These were available in a series of five and included a piano player with a guitarist, a drummer with a saxophone player, and three sets of dancers, one of which featured two couples. The figures were essentially "pottery cut-outs" on a flat base, much like a menu holder. The marketing of them suggested that they should be placed near the buyers radio, to view when listening to dance music. Unfortunately, they did not sell well and few examples remain today. They are, however, much sought after by collectors and hold the world record for Clarice Cliff prices.

In the same year, Clarice also introduced the Stamford shape. The Stamford teapot is a very Art Deco shape and was based on a design by Tetard Freres, the French silversmiths. The teapot was very successful and can be found decorated in many patterns. Examples today are expensive and never fail to receive admiring and envious glances at Art Deco fairs.

Above: Bowl in Spring Crocus. *Courtesy of Decodance.* $320.

Right: Preserve Pot in Crocus. *Courtesy of Decodance.* $320.

Lotus Jugs. Top row: Orange Luxor, Melon, and Swirls. Bottom row: Picasso Flower, Castellated Circle, and Farmhouse. *Photograph by and Courtesy of Bonhams, London UK/Bridgeman Art Library.* $2500-6000.

Another highly innovative shape followed in the form of the Conical sugar shaker. This is a shape that displays patterns exceptionally well and, because of its easy to accommodate small size, is very collectible.

Further shapes included the Art Nouveau inspired Daffodil and the hugely successful Bon Jour. The latter was again inspired by a Tetard Freres design. Bon Jour was unlike previous designs in that it was based entirely on circles and proved to be a major seller. In contrast to the circular form of Bon Jour, Clarice also de-

signed her oblong square edged Biaritz plates. These were integrated with Bon Jour pieces to form sets and were very successful.

Popular patterns of the year were Coral Firs, Honolulu, and Secrets. Honolulu, with its exotic sounding name, featured a different form of banding comprised of a series of black rings.

In 1934, Clarice became involved in the Artists for Industry project. This project entailed various designers of the day—including Dame Laura Knight and Dod Procter—submitting designs for production by Wilkinsons. The resulting pieces were exhibited at Harrods. Many of the designs were not typical of Clarice and, due to their high cost, the project was not commercially successful.

Bizarre patterns continued to be introduced in 1934, the most successful being Rhodanthe, which featured an etching technique. Clarice also made a last stand for the geometric/abstract cause, introducing Sungold, which quite ironically was very similar to her Original Bizarre designs.

However, the year also saw a departure for Clarice Cliff in her production of the non-Art Deco range of My Garden. The range generally consisted of a dreary colored body to the piece, with traditional moulded flowers to the base or handle. The range was enormously successful and probably marked the demise of the innovation and sheer afrontry of Bizarre and Fantasque.

By this time, public taste was now demanding much more restrained designs and Clarice turned her attention to simple teaware designs. During 1936, the word Bizarre was removed from the backstamp and this marked the end of an era for Clarice and the pottery buying public.

Lotus Jugs. Top row: Melon, Cubist, Cafe-au-lait Fruitburst. Bottom row: Floreat, Diamonds, and Mondrian. *Photograph by and Courtesy of Bonhams, London UK/Bridgeman Art Library.* $1600-6000.

A Clarice Cliff Stamford shape Teapot in the Ravel pattern. The shape of the Teapot was influenced by a design of Jean Tetard, the French Silversmith. *Photograph by and courtesy of David Smith.* $950.

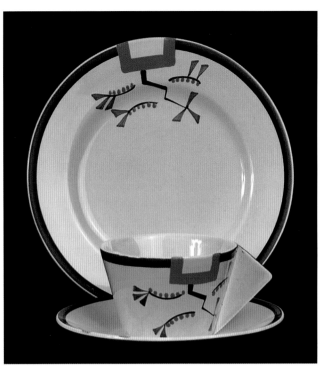

Conical Trio in the Ravel pattern. One of Clarice's more restrained and sophisticated cubist influenced patterns. *Courtesy of Decodance.* $325.

Three Vases in the Football pattern. Left: Shape 386, Middle: Goblet Shape 363, Right: Shape 369. The vase on the left features an unusual small extra black square to the pattern. *Courtesy of Banana Dance.* $8000-12000.

The very Deco shaped Double Conical Vase in the Blue W pattern. The shape allowed water to be held on two levels. *Photograph by and Courtesy of Bonhams, London UK/Bridgeman Art Library.* $7000+.

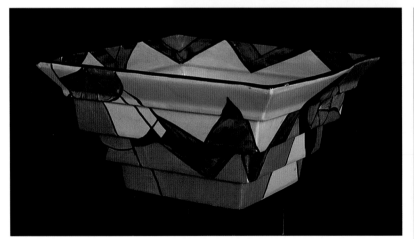

Above: A Stepped Bowl shape 417 in the Blue W pattern. *Courtesy of Banana Dance.* NP

Right: Shape 358 Vase in the Diamonds pattern. *Courtesy of Banana Dance.* $3000+.

Conical Early Morning Set in Diamonds pattern.
Courtesy of Banana Dance. $7000+.

Left: Blue W Sandwich Plate, 9 inches, $1400. Right: Picasso Flower
Sandwich Plate, 10.5 inches, marked Bizarre and dated May 1930, $800.
Photograph by and Courtesy of Bonhams, London UK/Bridgeman Art Library

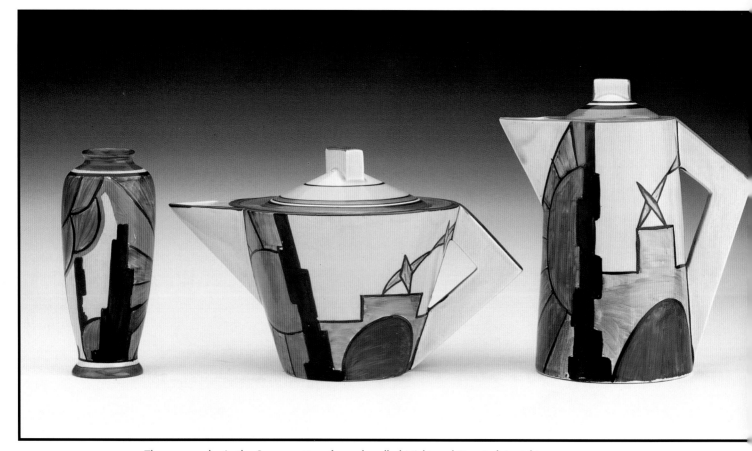

Three examples in the Sunray pattern formerly called Night and Day. Left to right: Shape 186, 5.5 inch Vase, $1600+. Conical Teapot, $3000+. Conical Coffeepot, $3000+. *Photograph by and Courtesy of Bonhams, London UK/Bridgeman Art Library.*

A set of four Age of Jazz figures, comprising of Drummer and Saxophone Player, Piano Player and Guitarist, Double Dancer, and a Single Couple. The figures were intended to be placed around a radio to enhance the ambiance when listening to dance music. They epitomize the era and are highly sought after today. Unfortunately they did not sell well at the time and are now extremely rare. Consequently they are very expensive. *Courtesy of Banana Dance.* $15000+ each.

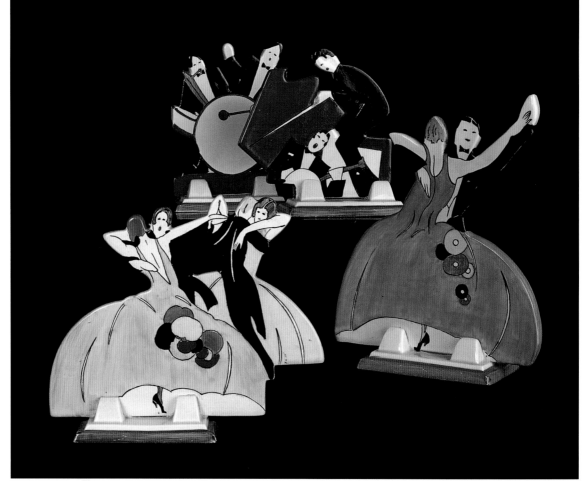

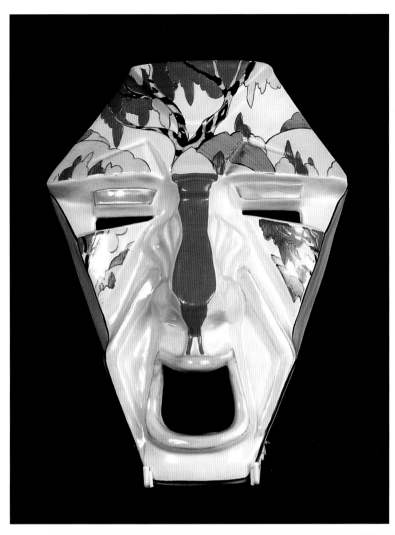

Left: A unique Grotesque Wall Mask in Honolulu. Signed by Ron Birks, who was employed at the Wilkinsons factory and designed the mask for Clarice. The mask was issued in patterns including Orange Secrets and Inspiration. This example in Honolulu is probably the only one in the world. *Courtesy of Banana Dance.* $10,000+.

Below: Bonjour Sugar Shaker and Vase in the Honolulu pattern. *Courtesy of Banana Dance.* $2000 + each.

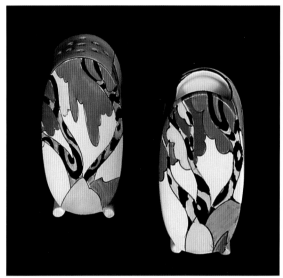

Three Vases in Honolulu. Left: Shape 212, Middle: Meiping, Right: Stepped Shape 366. *Courtesy of Banana Dance.* $2250-6000 each.

Honolulu Bonjour Double Candle Stick.
Courtesy of Banana Dance. $6000+.

Flanged Vase Shape 465 in Honolulu.
Courtesy of Banana Dance. $4000+.

A Biaritz shape Plate in Honolulu pattern.
Courtesy of Banana Dance. $1800+.

Cylindrical Jam Pot in the
Honolulu pattern. *Courtesy
of Banana Dance*. $1200+.

Left: Lido Lady Ashtrays Shape 561. It was available in two sizes, the larger of which is shown. The young lady is holding a towel and wearing beach pajamas. The ashtray to the left features the Orange Chintz pattern. *Courtesy of Banana Dance.* $3500+ each.

Below: An exceptionally rare Eton shape Coffee Set in the Cafe pattern (formally called "Cubes"). In view of the "mortarboard" type lid, the shape is probably named after the famous English Public School. The pattern was available in Cafe Red and Cafe Orange. *Courtesy of Banana Dance.* $12000+.

Coffee Set in the Tankard shape and Double V pattern, c. 1929.
Coffeepot, $1100; Milk and Sugar, $550; Individual Coffee
Cans and Saucers, $500. *Courtesy of Decodance.*

Fernpot by Clarice Cliff in the
Double V pattern, 3 inches high.
Courtesy of Decodance. $500.

Ashtray by Clarice Cliff in the
Double V pattern. *Courtesy of
Decodance.* $450.

A Meiping Vase, Shape 14 in the
Secrets pattern, height 6 inches.
Courtesy of Decodance. $1000.

Octagonal Cake Plate in the Secrets
pattern, with EPNS handle. *Courtesy
of Decodance.* $475.

A Daffodil shape Milk Jug in the Secrets
pattern. Marked Bizarre and Pattern No.
6070, c. 1933. *Courtesy of Decodance.* $450.

The Secrets pattern shown on a 4 inch Honey
Pot. Marked Bizare and Fantasque and painter's
mark "E". *Courtesy of Decodance.* $900.

A selection of items in the Secrets pattern. *Courtesy of Decodance.* $450-800.

Ashtray by Clarice Cliff in the Secrets pattern. *Courtesy of Decodance.* $400.

A 9 inch Plate in the Secrets pattern by Clarice Cliff, said to be one of her favorite patterns. *Courtesy of Decodance.* $700.

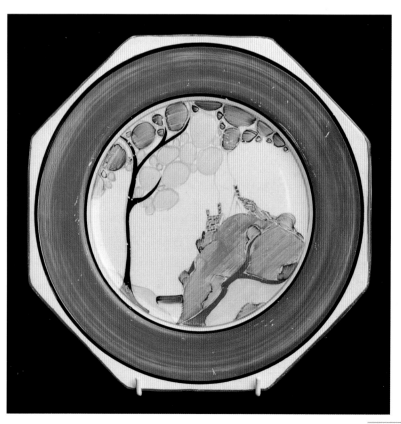

Above: A small Coaster in Orange Secrets. *Courtesy of Decodance.* $300.

Right: Octagonal Plate in Orange Secrets, otherwise known as "Seven Color Secrets." *Courtesy of Decodance.* $800.

Above: Bonjour Early Morning Set in the Stroud pattern. *Courtesy of Decodance.* $1500.

Right: An Athens Jug in Lydiat pattern. *Courtesy of Decodance.* $475.

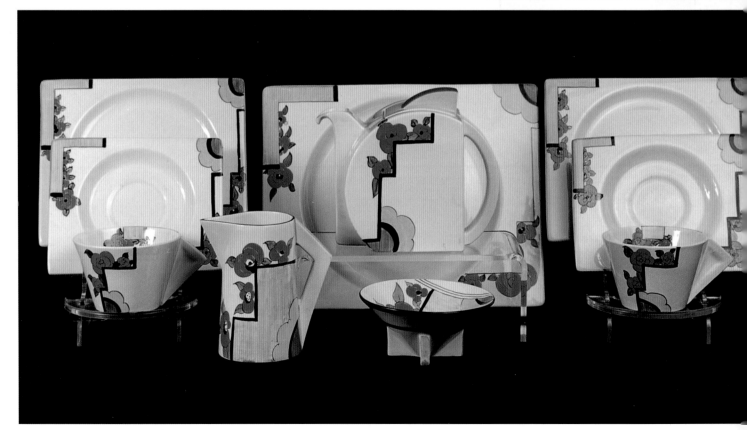

A part Tea Set in the Newport pattern: Stamford Teapot $1500, Conical Milk Jug $500, Conical Sugar $500, Trios, $575 each. *Courtesy of Decodance.*

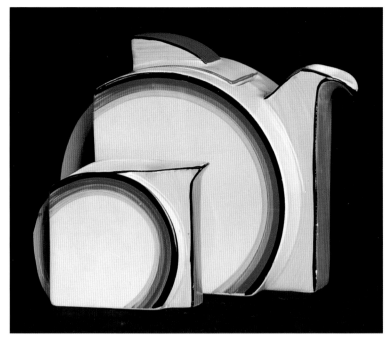

A Stamford shape Teapot and Milk Jug.
Courtesy of Decodance. $750 and $180.

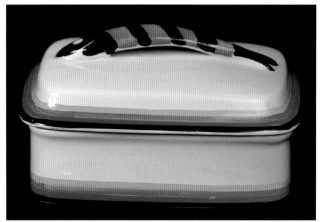

A Sardine Box, Shape 447. The Sardine on the top of the box is arched to form the handle. It was introduced around 1930 and became available in many patterns including Autumn, Carpet and Crocus. This banded example $350 and considerably more for an allover pattern. *Courtesy of Decodance.*

Marlene Wall Mask by Clarice Cliff. *Courtesy of Decodance.* $600.

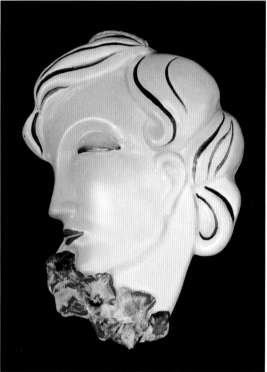

One of a series of small Face Masks by Clarice Cliff. Made in c. 1936, they are now quite rare and difficuld to find. As well as being intended for wall hanging, they were used as pendants. The example shown is 5.5 inches high and marked with a "Clarice Cliff" backstamp and shape number "787-1". *Courtesy of Decodance.* $500.

Wall Masks by Clarice Cliff. Top: Large Flora Mask, 14.5 inches high, $1900. Bottom Left: Flora, 6.75 inches high, $450. Bottom Right: Marlene, 6.5 inches high, $550. *Photograph by and Courtesy of Bonhams, London UK/Bridgeman Art Library.*

Bonjour shape Jam Pot in Coral Firs pattern.
Courtesy of Decodance. $800.

A large Biaritz Meat Platter in Coral Firs, $750, together with
a Biarritz/Bonjour Trio, $500. *Courtesy of Decodance.*

A Biaritz Plate with the full pattern of
Coral Firs. *Courtesy of Decodance.* $950.

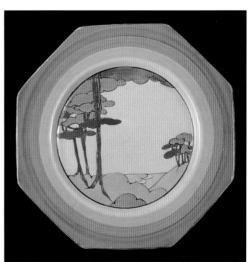

Clarice Cliff Octagonal Plate in the
Coral Firs pattern. *Courtesy of
Decodance.* $500.

A selection of items in the Blue Firs pattern, the rarer colorway of Coral Firs. Shoulder pattern Biaritz Plates in various sizes, $450-$700. Full pattern Plate, 10 inches, $1400. Front row Soup Dish with Underplate, $500, Conical part Coffee Set, $3800, Bonjour Shape Tureen $650. *Photograph by and Courtesy of Bonhams, London UK/Bridgeman Art Library*

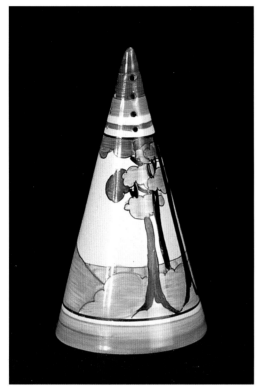

Conical Sugar Shaker in Blue Firs.
Courtesy of Banana Dance. $3000+.

Above: An Advertising Plaque in Blue Firs, size 3.25 x 2.25 inches. These small plaques were given to shops to use in their advertising displays. The rear is marked "Blue Firs by Clarice Cliff". *Courtesy of Banana Dance*. $3000+.

Right: Rear detail of the Advertising Plaque. *Courtesy of Banana Dance*.

Blue Firs shoulder pattern on a Biarritz Plate. $475.

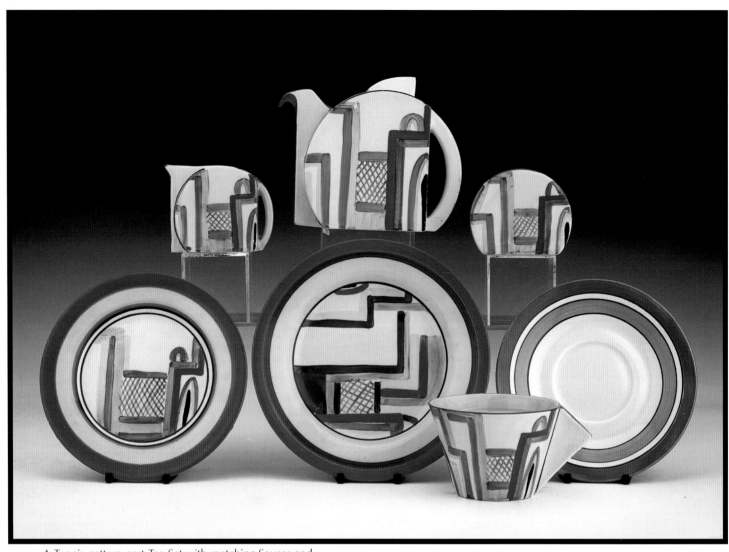

A Tennis pattern part Tea Set with matching Saucer and
extra Plate. *Photograph by and Courtesy of Bonhams,
London UK/Bridgeman Art Library.* $6000.

A Conical Cup and Saucer in the Rudyard
pattern. This is the alternative colorway of
Honolulu. *Courtesy of Banana Dance.* $600+.

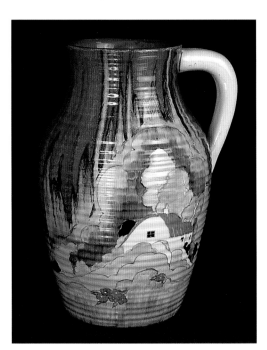

Lotus Jug in Forest Glen. The background sky is created by the Delecia painting technique. *Courtesy of Banana Dance*. $3000+.

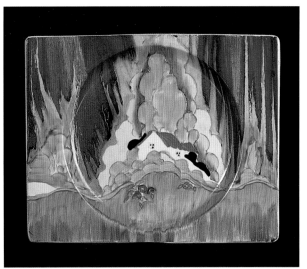

A Biaritz shape Plate in Forest Glen. The pattern was one of the last to be issued under the Bizarre range. *Courtesy of Banana Dance*. $1800+.

A Biarritz shape Plate with a shoulder pattern in Forest Glen. *Courtesy of Decodance*. $320.

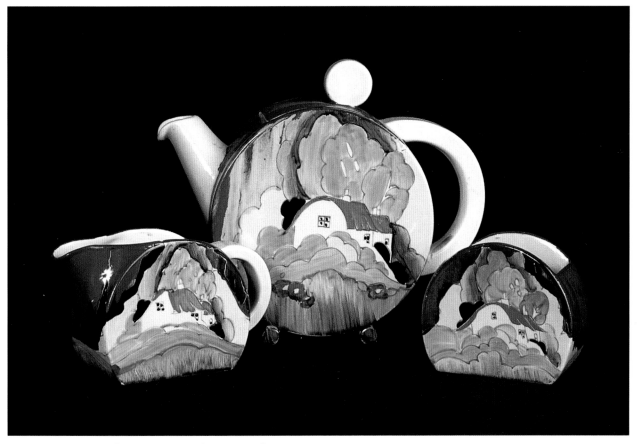

A Bonjour Teapot, Milk and Sugar Bowl in Forest Glen. *Courtesy of Banana Dance*. $3000+.

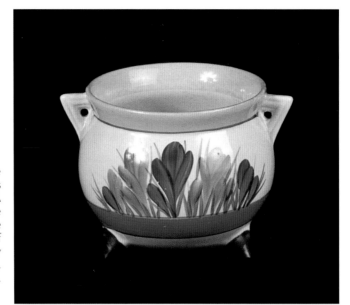

A Cauldron in the Blue Crocus pattern. A traditional shape with one of the rarer colorways of Crocus. *Courtesy of Banana Dance.* $450+.

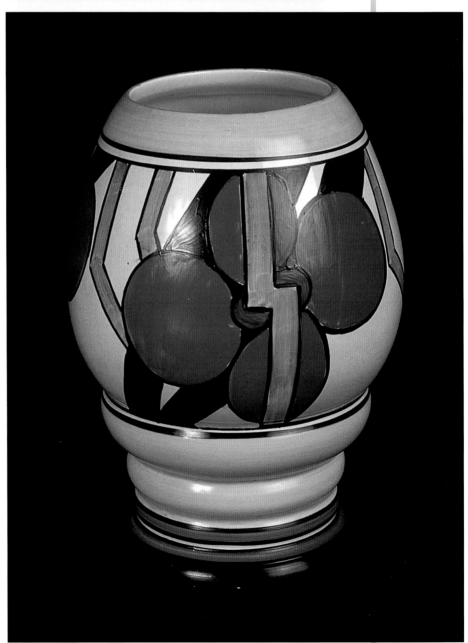

Picasso Flower pattern shown on a Shape 362 Vase. *Courtesy of Banana Dance.* NP

Above: An 18 inch Charger in the Pine Grove pattern. The scale of the piece is shown by the Dunhill Lighter at the bottom of the picture. *Courtesy of Decodance.* $2250.

Left: A Leda shaped Plate by Clarice Cliff in the Pine Grove pattern. *Courtesy of Decodance.* $450.

An Octagonal Bowl in the Swirls pattern. 8 inches diameter, 4 inches high. *Courtesy of Decodance.* $1000.

Plate in the Swirls pattern. This pattern is very similar to the book cover of *A History of Caricature* by Bohun Lynch published in 1926. *Courtesy of Decodance.* $1200.

Jam Pot by Clarice Cliff in the Swirls pattern. *Courtesy of Decodance.* $900.

A 9 inch Plate with a full patterned version of Capri, c. 1936. *Courtesy of Decodance.* $350.

Above: A Milano Vase in Shape No. 341, height 5 inches. The style is restrained and minimalist and reminiscent of Keith Murray. *Courtesy of Decodance.* $300.

Right: A Scraphito Lamp Base by Clarice Cliff. *Courtesy of Decodance.* $450.

Bowl with Sharks Tooth pattern. 6.5 inches diameter. *Courtesy of Decodance.* $600.

Bowl in the Sungold pattern, 9 inch diameter. The piece is painted internally and externally. *Courtesy of Decodance.* $650.

Honeypot, 4 inch high in the Sungold pattern. Marked Bizarre, c. 1934. *Courtesy of Decodance.* $850.

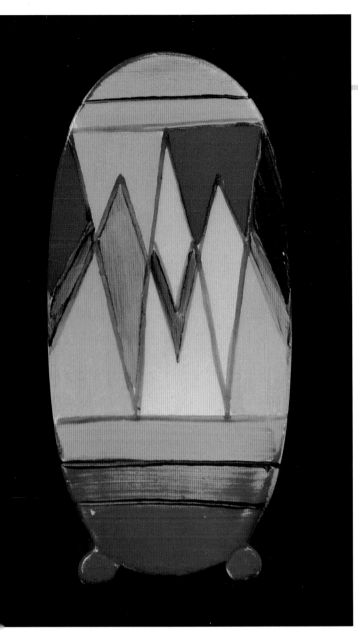

Left: A Bonjour Sugar Shaker in the Sungold pattern. *Courtesy of Decodance.* $1200.

Below: Octagonal Plate in Sungold. *Courtesy of Decodance.* $600.

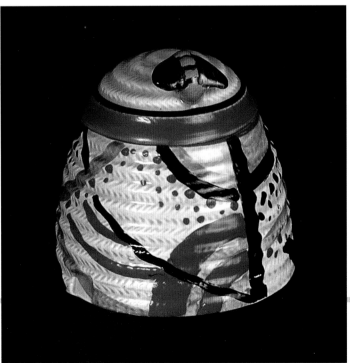

A very rare Honeypot in the Carpet pattern. *Courtesy of Banana Dance*. $1500+.

Top: A Perth Jug in the Woodland pattern. *Courtesy of Decodance.* $550.

Center: A Woodland pattern Tea Set, made up with Athens shape Teapot $850, Conical Cups and Saucers $450, small Plates $300, large Plate $450. *Courtesy of Decodance.*

Bottom: A Sandwich Tray in the Woodland pattern. *Courtesy of Decodance.* $700.

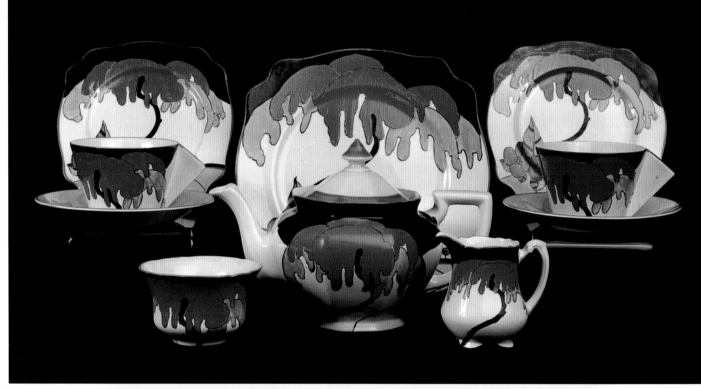

Above: Unusually, the Saucer from the Woodland Tea Set has the pattern continued onto it, as opposed to being merely decorated with Banding.

Left: Isis Jug in the Sliced Fruit pattern, c. 1930. *Courtesy of Decodance.* $1200.

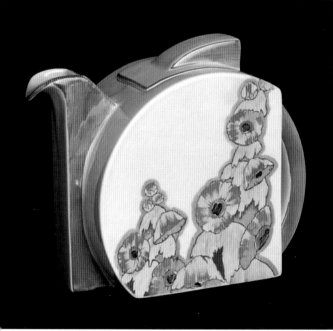

Above: Stamford shape Teapot in the Sunshine pattern. *Courtesy of Decodance.* $950.

Right: Fernpot in Petunia, the alternative colorway of Canterbury Bells. *Courtesy of Decodance.* $450.

A traditionally shaped Jug with the avant-garde Lightning pattern. *Courtesy of Banana Dance.* $1500+.

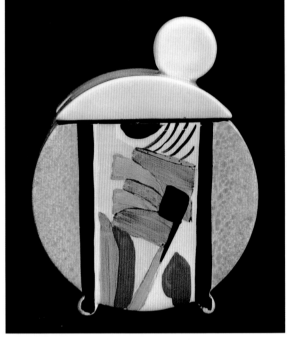

Bonjour Jam Pot in the Xavier pattern. An abstract design on a Cafe-au-Lait background, c. 1932. *Photograph by and courtesy of Harold and Maureen.* $850.

Above: A Biarritz Plate in the Aurea pattern. *Courtesy of Decodance.* $300.

Right: A Conical Sugar Shaker in Aurea. *Courtesy of Decodance.* $750.

An unusual Ashtray in the Viscaria pattern, c. 1936. Note the holes around the rim for cigarettes and matches. *Courtesy of Decodance.* $300.

Above: A Jug in Aurea. *Courtesy of Decodance.* $400.

Left: The Rodanthe pattern shown on an Inverted Bowl. *Courtesy of Decodance.* $375.

A Tray depicting the Viscaria pattern. *Courtesy of Decodance.* $300.

FANTASQUE

In 1929, the profits from the sale of Bizarre Ware were so great that Colley Shorter decided to transfer some of the sales to the adjoining Wilkinsons factory in order to minimize his tax liability. To achieve this, some of Clarice Cliff's patterns were issued under the range name of Fantasque and were attributed to the Wilkinsons factory. Clarice herself had a slightly different explanation for the introduction of the new range, "Bizarre was usually sold to one customer (shop) in a town, so Fantasque was supposed to be a little different and sold to another shop."[4]

The Fantasque range was sold contemporaneously with the Bizarre range at a slightly higher price. Fantasque was combined with many of Clarice's new shapes, including the Stamford and Conical ranges and it was highly successful. To accompany the range, a new backstamp was introduced, "Fantasque hand painted by Clarice Cliff".

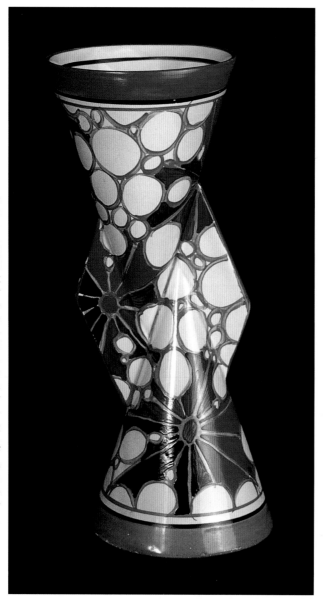

Yo Yo Vase (Shape 379) in Broth, 9.25 inches high. Marked Fantasque and with a gilt Lawley's retailer mark. The shape is perhaps the most outrageously designed of Clarice's vases. Yet, when analysed, it is a clever, but fairly simple amalgamation of two inverted cones. Broth was one of the first patterns to be issued in the Fantasque range. *Courtesy of Banana Dance.* $8000+.

The first patterns in the range included Broth, Caprice, Kandina, Cherries, Lily, and Fruit. Further patterns were swiftly designed, one of which was Trees and House, the first of the classic Clarice Cliff landscapes. Another was the Melon pattern, a cubist type stylized fruit pattern. Other early Fantasque patterns were Mountain, Umbrellas and Rain, Sunrise, and Gardenia.

In 1931, two of the classic Clarice Cliff patterns became available. Summerhouse was a bright surreal landscape with yellow trees, black bushes, and a red native-like hut. The more successful of the two patterns, however, was Autumn—previously known by collectors as "Balloon Trees" until the real name was discovered. The Autumn pattern has a cartoon-like landscape with trees featuring sinuous trunks and multicolored foliage, together with a cottage, and grass in the most adventurous of colors. The pattern was very successful and sold in great quantities. Despite its wide availability today, Autumn is relatively expensive to acquire due to its desirability with collectors.

Even though the early thirties was a period in which Britain was strangled by the Depression and unemployment was at twenty percent in the Potteries, Clarice went from strength to strength.

The year 1931 also saw the introduction of the Gibraltar and House and Bridge patterns. Gibralter was somewhat of a departure for Clarice from her previous patterns; relying on gentle pastels as opposed to her usual strident colors. House and Bridge was a typical Clarice Cliff landscape. It was known by collectors for many years as the Front Cover pattern because it was featured on the front of the first book to be written about Clarice Cliff.[5]

In 1932, the quintessential Clarice Cliff pattern, Orange Roof Cottage, was added to the Fantasque range. This is probably the landscape pattern most widely associated with Clarice Cliff.

A later pattern, that has great significance for collectors is May Avenue. This pattern is named after a street close to Clarice's family home in Tunstall, although it is clearly taken from a painting by Amadeo Modigliani called Landscape at Cagnes. The pattern is extremely rare and is the most expensive to acquire, holding world records for the sale of a conical sugar shaker and a Bon Jour tea for two.

By 1934, the public taste was changing toward more subtly decorated tableware. Consequently, the demand for Fantasque patterns decreased and they were phased out.

Left: The Trees and House pattern shown on a Conical Teapot, $1500, Conical Milk Jug, $350, and a Beaker, $400. *Photograph Courtesy of Bona Arts Decorative Ltd.*

Below: A Plate and Hiawatha Bowl in Orange Trees and House, $600 and $1200 respectively; together with an Ashtray and Sabot in Orange Picasso Flower, $400 and $600 respectively. *Photograph Courtesy of Bona Arts Decorative Ltd.*

Top: Conical Pitcher in Gardenia, $1200. Shape 342 Vase in Melons, $1800. *Photograph Courtesy of Bona Arts Decorative Lt*

Above: A Bowl in the Melons pattern. 8.5 inch diameter, marked Fantasque and Bizarre. *Courtesy of Decodance.* $600.

Right: A 10 inch diameter Plate in Fantasque Wax Flower. *Courtesy of Decodance.* $650.

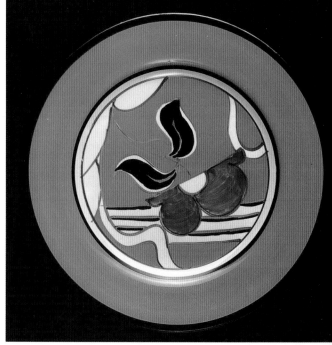

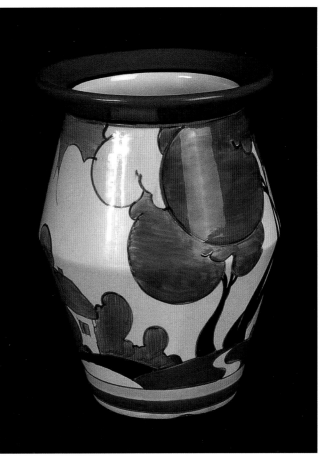

Above: Jam Pot in the Fruitburst pattern. *Courtesy of Decodance.* $450.

Right: A Shape 342 Vase in the Blue Autumn pattern. *Courtesy of Banana Dance.* $3000+.

Below: Cake Plate with metal handle in the Blue Autumn pattern. *Courtesy of Decodance.* $650.

Above: An Isis Vase featuring the Autumn pattern. Note the unusual green and Appliqué Banding. *Courtesy of Banana Dance*. $6000+.

Above right: A 7 inch Plate in Red Autumn marked Fantasque. The first and the rarest of the Autumn colorways. *Courtesy of Decodance*. $700.

Right: Orange Autumn Plate. *Courtesy of Decodance*. $750.

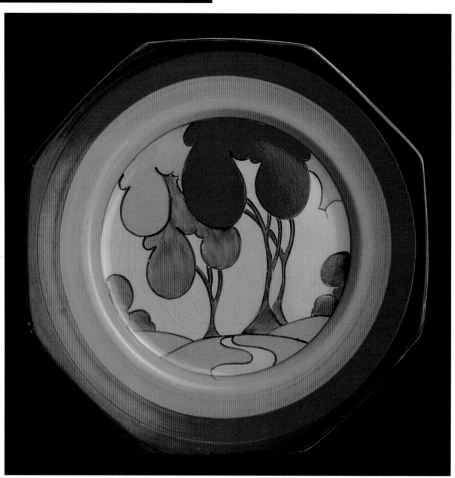

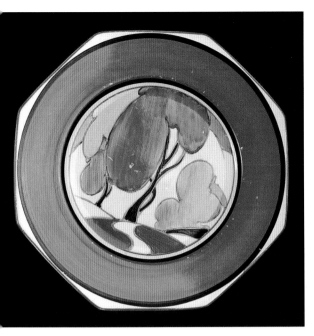

Above: Octagonal Plate in Blue Autumn. *Courtesy of Decodance.* $750.

Right: A 10 inch Plate showing the Pastel Autumn pattern. *Courtesy of Decodance.* $1000.

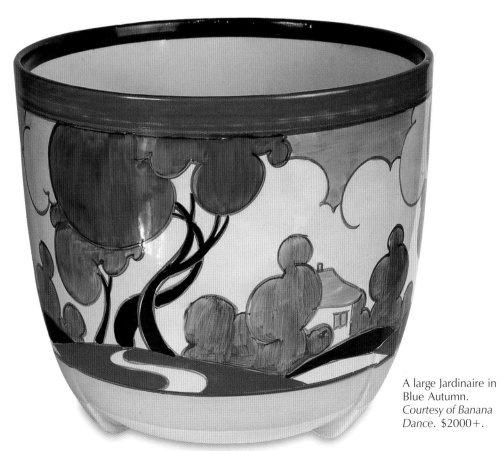

A large Jardinaire in Blue Autumn. *Courtesy of Banana Dance.* $2000+.

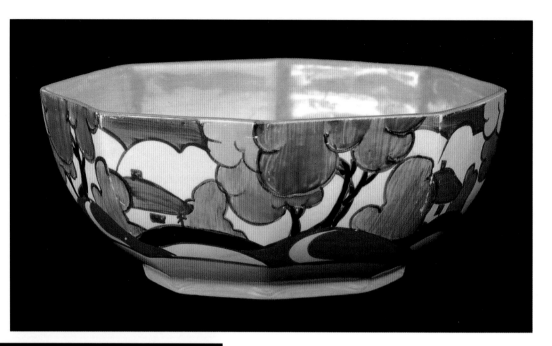

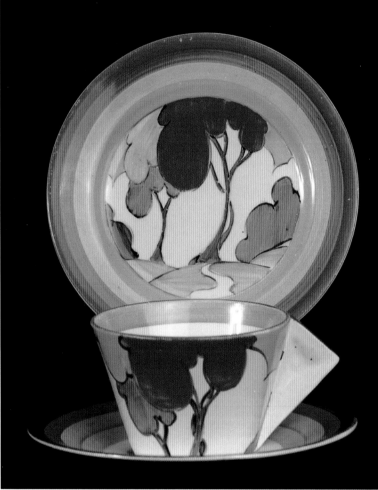

Above: Octagonal Bowl in Blue Autumn. *Courtesy of Decodance.* $750.

Left: Conical Cup and Saucer with full pattern Plate in Orange Autumn. *Courtesy of Decodance.* $900.

Below: Teapot Stand by Clarice Cliff in the Orange Autumn pattern. *Courtesy of Decodance.* $450.

Athens shape Teapot in Blue Autumn.
Courtesy of Decodance. $900.

A Sugar Bowl with EPNS Lid in the Autumn
pattern. *Courtesy of Decodance.* $375.

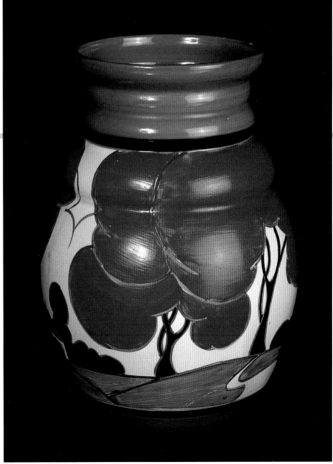

Shape 369 Vase in Red Autumn, c. 1931. This very Art
Deco shape was one of the first shapes designed by
Clarice and was influenced by the French designer
Robert Lallemant. *Courtesy of Banana Dance.* NP

Shape 358 Vase in Red Autumn.
Courtesy of Banana Dance. NP

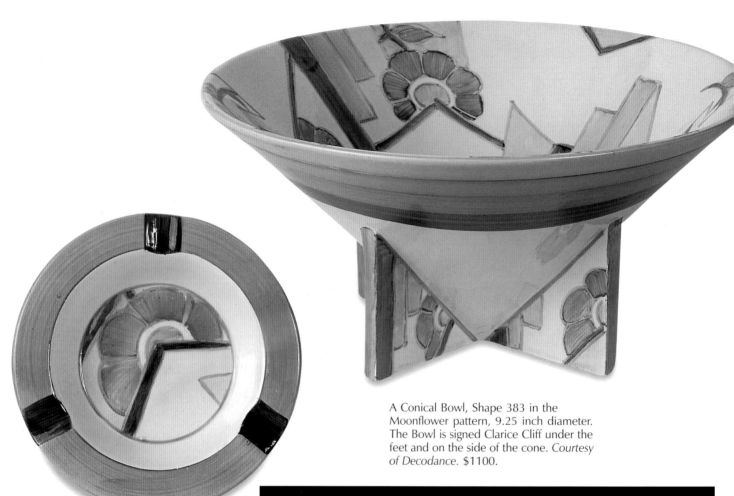

A Conical Bowl, Shape 383 in the Moonflower pattern, 9.25 inch diameter. The Bowl is signed Clarice Cliff under the feet and on the side of the cone. *Courtesy of Decodance.* $1100.

Ashtray in the Moonflower pattern, 4.5 inch diameter. *Courtesy of Decodance.* $400.

An Octagonal Plate in the Moonflower pattern. *Courtesy of Decodance.* $650.

A cylindrical Jam Pot with the Gilbralter pattern, 3.5 inches high, Shape No. 3. *Courtesy of Decodance.* $1200.

A selection of shapes in the Gilbralter pattern. *Photograph by and Courtesy of Bonhams, London UK/Bridgeman Art Library.* $650-2800.

A Gilbralter pattern Conical Early Morning Set. Marked Bizarre and Fantasque. Teapot impressed with the number "42." This number refers to how many teapots could be fired together in the oven, and therefore the smaller the number, the larger the teapot. *Photograph by and Courtesy of Bonhams, London UK/Bridgeman Art Library.* $6000.

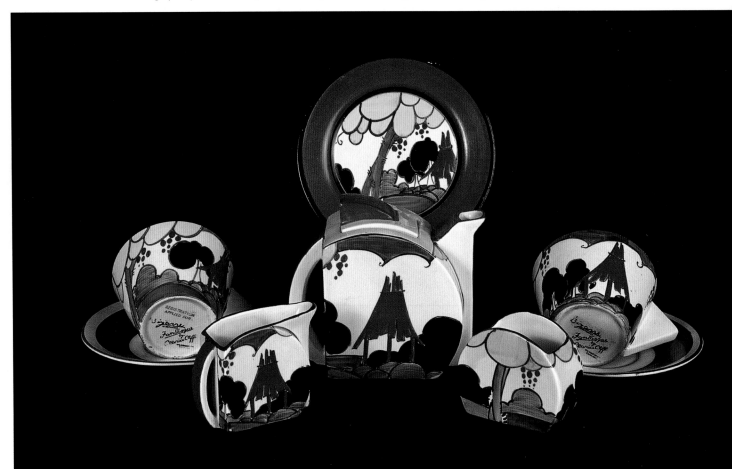

A Stamford Early Morning Set in the Summerhouse pattern. *Courtesy of Banana Dance.* $6000+.

An Eve Bowl in Summerhouse.
Courtesy of Banana Dance. NP

Shape 358 Vase in Summerhouse.
Courtesy of Banana Dance. NP

The rear pattern detail of the Summerhouse
Vase. *Courtesy of Banana Dance.*

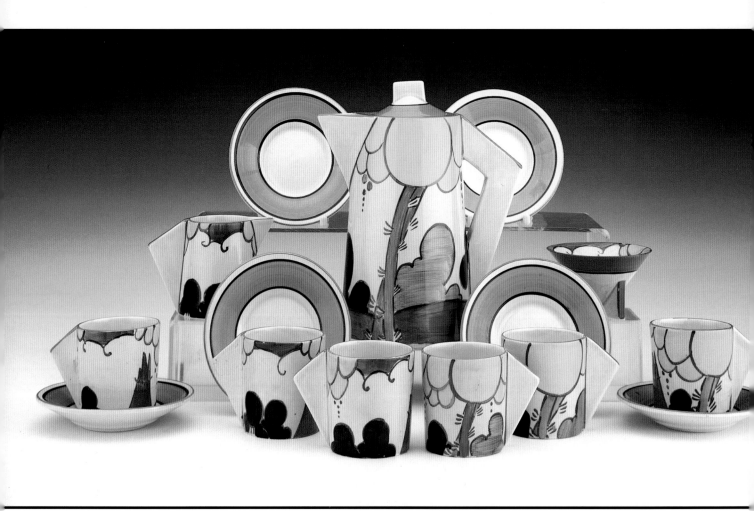

Above: A Summerhouse pattern Conical Coffee Set. Marked Fantasque. *Photograph by and Courtesy of Bonhams, London UK/Bridgeman Art Library.* $6500.

Right: A giant 16.25 inch high Meiping Vase in House and Bridge. *Photograph by and Courtesy of Bonhams, London UK/Bridgeman Art Library.* $12000+.

Shape 365 Vase featuring House and Bridge pattern. *Courtesy of Banana Dance.* NP

A Wall Plate in House and Bridge pattern. The pattern was formerly known as "Front Cover" as it was featured on the front of the first Clarice Cliff book. *Courtesy of Banana Dance.* $1500+.

A Stamford Teapot, Milk Jug and Sugar Bowl in House and Bridge. Notice how the paintress has cleverly continued the pattern on all three pieces. *Courtesy of Banana Dance.* $4500+

Above: Vases shown in the Orange House pattern. Left: Shape 356 with red banding, Middle: Shape 356 with green banding, Right: Shape 358 with orange banding. The usual banding is green or yellow. The example shown with red banding is unique and the only known example. *Courtesy of Banana Dance.* NP

Right: An Athens Jug in the Green House pattern. *Courtesy of Banana Dance.* NP

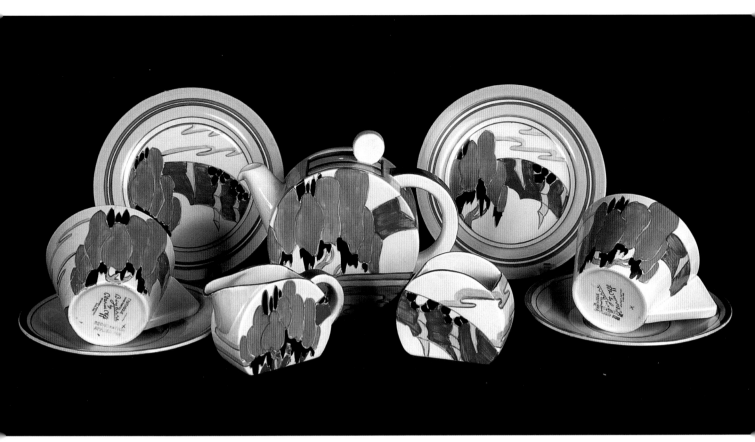

Above: Bonjour Tea Set in the Solitude pattern. The teapot skillfully includes the whole of the pattern on the front and the bridge passes under the handle to be featured on the back. The set unsually includes two plates. *Courtesy of Banana Dance.* $6000+.

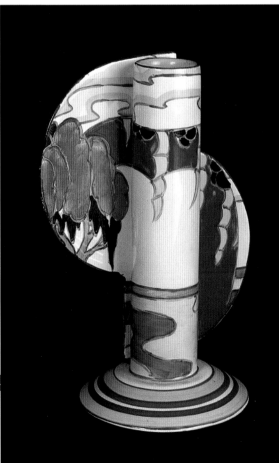

Left: Shape 464 Flower Tube Vase in Solitude. The rear of the vase is a flat surface and typically of Clarice is also decorated. *Courtesy of Banana Dance.* NP

Left: The Quintissential Clarice Cliff Landscape pattern Orange Roof Cottage, shown on a Shape 365 Vase. Middle: Conical Sugar Shaker. Right: The rarer colorway of Pink Roof Cottage on a Shape 187 Vase. *Courtesy of Banana Dance.* $3000+ for the Sugar Shaker.

Circular Plate in the Kew pattern. *Courtesy of Banana Dance.* NP

A pair of Candlesticks in the Sunrise pattern. *Photograph by and Courtesy of Sotheby's.* $2000.

APPLIQUÉ

In 1930, Clarice Cliff chose the French word "Appliqué," literally translated meaning "applied," for a separate range of pottery. Many of the patterns to be issued in the range were also to have continental names.

The designs were decorated using two new techniques. Instead of the usual permanent outlining, commonly seen on Bizarre and Fantasque pieces, the outlining was done with Indian Ink. This meant that, when the piece was fired, the ink was burnt off, leaving a decoration that showed no outlining. Also, unlike many Bizarre and Fantasque patterns where the Honeyglaze of the piece is used to form part of the pattern, Appliqué pieces were painted all over the visible parts. Also, more costly paints were used for the range.

After she returned from Paris in 1927, Clarice acquired some prints of the work of Edouard Benedictus, and these provided the inspiration for the first two patterns in the range. In March 1930, Lucerne and Lugano were introduced; Lucerne depicted a castle landscape and Lugano a water wheel. The sky on both patterns was originally colored in blue. However, due to production problems or to make the patterns more "familiar," the color of the sky was within a couple of months changed to orange.

Additional patterns added to the range in 1930 were Avignon, Windmill, Garden, Palermo, Red Tree, Caravan, and Bird of Paradise. In 1931, Monsoon, Etna, and Eden were also added. This year also saw the introduction of Idyll, a rather untypical Clarice pattern featuring a sugary Crinoline Lady in a garden scene. The pattern is incongruous with the rest of the Appliqué range, not only because of its subject matter, but because it did not feature the "all over" paint technique. It was, however, a good seller and was later transferred to the Fantasque range.

The backstamp of the range included the word "Appliqué," hand painted up to 1931 and printed after that date. Due to the high cost of Appliqué, it did not sell particularly well and examples are therefore quite rare today. Consequently, prices are generally very expensive.

An impressive group of Appliqué Ware. *Photograph Courtesy of "Bona" Arts Decorative Ltd.*

A small Dessert Plate in Appliqué Blue Lucerne. Hand-written Appliqué mark. The pattern was only issued in the Blue colorway (determined by the color of the sky) for a few months. After that, it was issued with an Orange sky. Although the Blue colorway was issued again later with a lighter Blue. *Courtesy of Decodance.* $1600.

A Mieping Vase in the Appliqué Red Tree pattern, c. 1930. *Courtesy of Banana Dance.* NP

Left: Lotus Jug in Appliqué Blue Lagano, 11.25 inches high, $9000. Back: Shape 341 Vase in Appliqué Blue Lugano, $2200. Front: A Conical Bowl, Shape 383, in Appliqué Blue Lucerne, $2400. Right: An Appliqué Avignon pattern Lotus Jug, 10 inches high, $6000. *Photograph by and Courtesy of Bonhams, London UK/Bridgeman Art Library.*

An Appliqué Blue Lucerne Preserve Pot in Shape 230.
Photograph by and Courtesy of Sotheby's. $1500.

Tray and Egg Cups in Appliqué Orange Lucerne.
Courtesy of Banana Dance. NP

Above: Appliqué Windmill Bowl.
Courtesy of Banana Dance. NP

Right: Inside detail of the Windwill Bowl. *Courtesy of Banana Dance.*

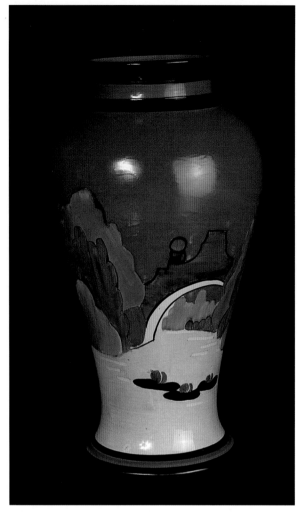

A large Meiping Vase in Appliqué Avignon. *Courtesy of Banana Dance.* NP

A Shape 200 Vase in Blossom. Although this is an early shape it shows a distinct Art Deco influence. The Blossom pattern is rare and is known from only five examples. *Courtesy of Banana Dance.* NP

The Idyll pattern shown on an Octaganol Cake Plate, $700, and a Shape 475 Daffodil Bowl, $1500. *Photograph Courtesy of Bona Arts Decorative Ltd.*

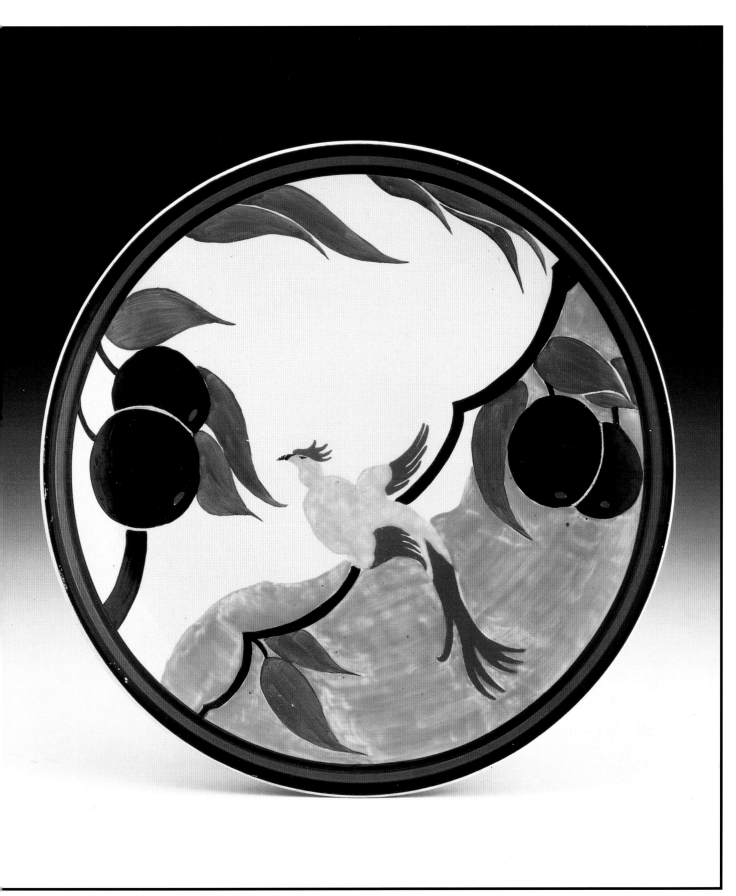

A 13 inch Charger in Appliqué Bird of Paradise. Possibly the only example in existence and probably painted by Clarice herself. *Photograph by and Courtesy of Bonhams, London UK/Bridgeman Art Library.* $6500.+

INSPIRATION

Inspiration is the name of an exclusive range of pottery introduced in 1929. It is very different to other Clarice Cliff designs. The pattern of the decoration is created, not by the usual method of hand-painting, but is made up of different colored matt glazes.

To produce the effect, each piece had to be fired twice, with metallic oxides applied to the surface. The result was very luxurious art pottery with stunning deep blues, lilacs, mauves, turquoises, and pinks. A press release at the time said that ... "Inspiration has created tremendous interest unveiling the secret (which was lost for centuries) of reproducing in a superb matt glaze that gorgeous colour peculiar to Ancient Egyptian Pottery, known as Scarab Blue."

Shapes used for the range include Lotus jugs, together with various traditional vase shapes. Inspiration was also applied to some of Clarice's more modern shapes, including the Yo Yo vase, square stepped bowls, shape 366 stepped vase, shape 370 globe vase, and conical coffee sets.

Patterns for the range include Inspiration versions of Persian, Caprice, Clouvre, Lily, Autumn, and the incongruous Knight Errant. Clarice also used the Inspiration range to promote the Bizarre range. She took Inspiration bowls, painted the words "Bizarre by Clarice Cliff" on the inside of the bowls, and used them for advertising displays.

Due to the complicated and time consuming techniques required to produce Inspiration, the range was at the time very expensive. Overall, it proved to be too costly for the buying public and was phased out in 1931.

The usual backstamp found on Inspiration pieces is handwritten and includes the word "Inspiration" in script

A selection of Inspiration pieces. The 13 inch Charger in Inspiration Caprice is taken from one of the first Landscape patterns designed by Clarice. *Photograph by and Courtesy of Bonhams, London UK/Bridgeman Art Library.* $450-4000.

A selection of items in Inspiration Persian. The Shape 264 Vase (top right) is an early painted version of the pattern. *Photograph by and Courtesy of Bonhams, London UK/Bridgeman Art Library.* $600-4000.

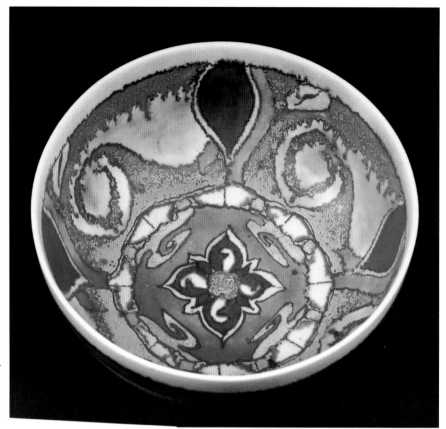

Bowl internally
decorated with
Inspiration Persian.
*Courtesy of
Decodance.* $1000.

Above: An Inspiration Shape 368
Fernpot. *Courtesy of Banana Dance.*
NP

Right: Lotus Jug in Inspiration Persian.
Courtesy of Decodance. $3000.

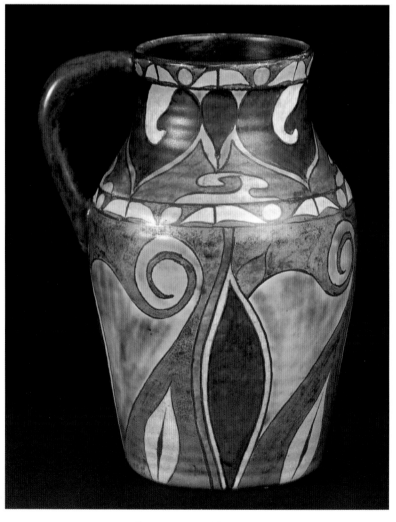

LATONA

Yet another exclusive range introduced by Clarice Cliff in 1929, Latona differed in that it used a milky colored glaze as opposed to the Honeyglaze used for Bizarre and Fantasque. New patterns were designed for the range including Latona Red Roses, Tree, Stained Glass, Dahlia, Aztec, Flowerheads, Orchid, and Rainbow Squares. Shapes used for the range were wall plaques, stepped bowls, conical tea and coffee sets, Stamford teaware, and Isis and Yo Yo vases.

An advertisement of the time claims, "Latona gives the full glory of modern colouring on beautiful, satiny, matt glazes of varying tones."

Although the range did not remain in production for many years, it was apparently successful and the most frequent found patterns today are Latona Red Roses and Dahlia.

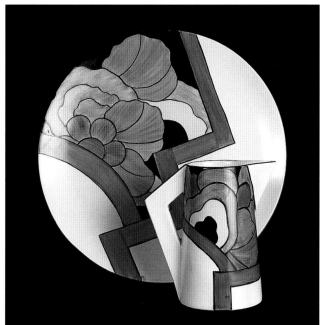

Above: A selection of Latona. Top row: Latona Blossom Plate, Latona Cartoon Flowers Vase Shape 264, Latona Oranges Dahlia single handled Lotus Jug. Bottom row: Latona Tree Shape 370 Globe Vase, Latona Tree Shape 383 Conical Bowl, Latona Dahlia Shape 369 Stepped Vase, Latona Tree Stepped Vase. *Photograph by and Courtesy of Bonhams, London UK/Bridgeman Art Library.* $800-4500.

Left: Wall Plate, 13", and Conical Jug in Latona Dahlia pattern. *Courtesy of Banana Dance.* NP

Latona Dahlia shown on a Shape 369 Stepped Vase. 7.5 inches high. *Courtesy of Banana Dance.* NP

Latona Red Roses: Wall Plaque, 13 inches, Isis Vase, 9.25 inches high, Shape 419 Bowl. *Photograph by and Courtesy of Bonhams, London UK/Bridgeman Art Library.* $600-3000.

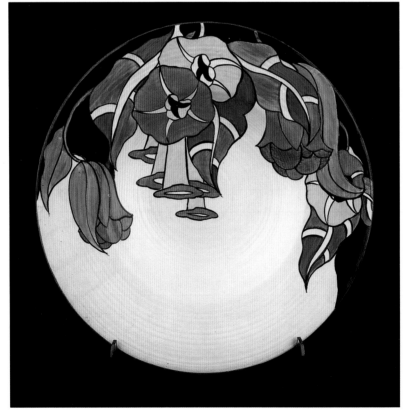

Latona Bouquet on an 18 inch wall Charger. *Photograph by and Courtesy of Bonhams, London UK/ Bridgeman Art Library.* $15000.

FANCIES

One of Clarice Cliff's ambitions was to become a sculptress and she used her modelling skills throughout her career. This obviously assisted her with the designs of vases and teaware, but it also encouraged her to design various "fancies." These are small, less essen-tial items and include bookends, pencil holders, sabots and inkwells.

The production of fancies, was an important source of revenue for Wilkinsons and their popularity, even at a time of general financial depression, is testament to the unique success of Clarice Cliff.

An extremely unusual figure in cubist form, featuring Original Bizarre decoration. *Courtesy of Banana Dance*. NP

A novelty Laughing Cat figure. This was based on a shape designed by Louis Wain. *Courtesy of Banana Dance*. $1500+.

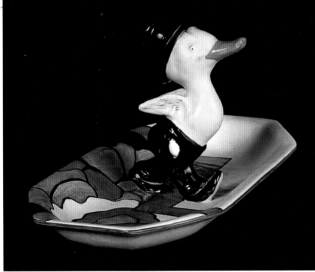

An amusing Mr. Puddleduck Sandwich Tray in the Latona Dahlia pattern. *Courtesy of Banana Dance*. NP

Golly and Teddy Bookends. *Courtesy of Banana Dance*. NP

AFTER BIZARRE

After 1936, backstamps omitted the words "Bizarre" and "Hand painted." Crocus continued to sell well and remained in production up to 1964. The My Garden range flourished. Rhodanthe was still very successful and further colorways were introduced. Masses of simple, restrained designs were applied to dinnerware that still utilised previous Art Deco shapes.

New landscape patterns such as Taormina and Stile and Trees were introduced and sold alongside Forest Glen, which had been released just prior to the demise of Bizarre.

Vases were introduced, that were miles apart from previous Deco shapes. They took the form of moulded ware depicting budgerigars and vine leaves. The hideous Celtic Harvest range saw the light of day, with its "Cement thrown" look.

In 1939, Colley's wife died and shortly after, Clarice found her own personal happiness. She married Colley in December 1940. After Colley died in 1963, Clarice inherited the factory were she had worked as a girl; but, in 1964 she sold it to the pottery firm of Midwinter. Thereafter, Clarice became rather reclusive until she died in 1972.

Pitcher in My Garden. Marked Bizarre. The range was issued in 1936 just prior to the demise of the Bizarre backstamp, so this is an early example. The range could not be described as being particularly Art Deco. It was, however, enormously successful. Alternative colorways for the body of the piece are Verdant and Flame. *Courtesy of Decodance.* $350.

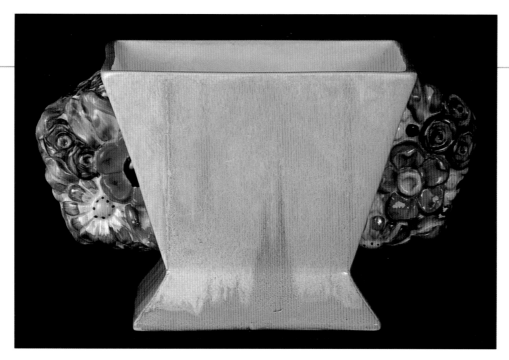

Above: A Clarice Cliff Vase in My Garden. Showing that traditional patterns continued to be combined with earlier Deco shapes. *Courtesy of Decodance.* $450.

Left: A Preserve Pot in Taormina. *Courtesy of Decodance.* $350.

Below: Book Vase by Clarice Cliff. Signed on the inside of the vase. The vase was issued in various sizes and generally featured a verse on the spine and cover. The example shown is rather more colorful than usual. *Courtesy of Decodance.* $375.

RENEWED INTEREST

In the early 1970s, Martin Battersby's book, *The Decorative Thirties*, featured examples of Clarice Cliff pottery. He later helped organise a Clarice Cliff exhibition at Brighton, England, in 1972, for which Clarice herself, contributed pieces. In America, Bevis Hillier included numerous Clarice Cliff pieces in his "World of Art Deco" exhibition, held at Minneapolis in 1971.

The first book on Clarice Cliff was written by Peter Wentworth-Shields and Kay Johnson in 1976. It was published by L'Odeon, a shop situated at Fulham High Street in London that pioneered the display and sale of Clarice Cliff.

In 1983, Christies took the bold step of holding the first ever sale devoted to Clarice Cliff. Such sales are now a permanent fixture of Christies' yearly calendar.

After acquiring the Wilkinsons factory, Midwinter, in 1985, issued a range of pieces hand painted with some of the classic Clarice Cliff patterns. These were issued as a limited edition and included a Mieping vase in Honolulu, a conical sugar shaker in House and Bridge, and a conical bowl in Umbrellas and Rain. They succeeded in capturing the essence of Clarice and had a backstamp that read "Royal Staffordshire Pottery by Clarice Cliff".

Midwinter was taken over by Wedgwood, the current owners of the Clarice Cliff copyright. In conjunction with The Clarice Cliff Collectors Club, Wedgwood has over the years also issued a series of limited edition hand painted pieces. These are collectible in themselves and feature a resurrected Bizarre backstamp.

One of the major driving forces behind today's interest in Clarice Cliff has been Len Griffin. He established the Clarice Cliff Collectors Club in 1981 and since then has devoted his life to the promotion and appreciation of Clarice Cliff. In 1988, together with Louis and Susan Meisel, he published the first authoritative book on Clarice Cliff called *The Bizarre Affair*.

Other notable books have included *Collecting Clarice Cliff* by Howard Watson and the superb *Rich Designs of Clarice Cliff* by Richard Green and Des Jones.

And to bring Clarice completely up to date, an excellent Web Site, mastered by Andrew Hutton and Dr. Phil Woodward, has now been established.

The work of the early pioneers, the commercial insight of Christies, and the never ending crusade of Len Griffin, have ensured that Clarice Cliff is today regarded as the most important Art Deco ceramic designer of the era.

After taking over the Wilkinsons factory, Midwinter released a series of Clarice Cliff re-issues. These included a vase in Honolulu, a conical bowl in Umbrellas and Rain and some conical sugar sifters. Shown here is the Sugar Sifter in House and Bridge which is marked "Royal Staffordshire Pottery by Clarice Cliff". The series managed to capture the essence of Clarice and are now highly collectible. *Courtesy of Decodance.* Sugar Sifter, $350.

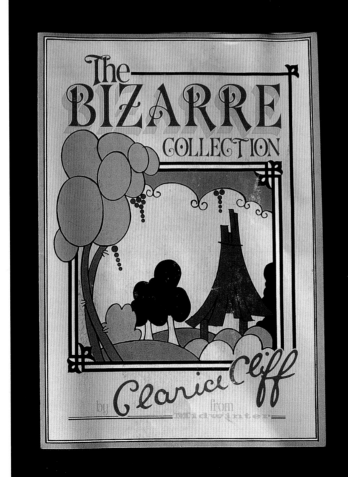

Left: Limited edition reproduction Age of Jazz figure by Wedgwood in the Latona Red Roses pattern. *Courtesy of Decodance.* $750.

Below: The Bizooka recreated by Wedgwood for The Clarice Cliff Centenary Exhibition 1999, held at The Wedgwood Museum, Stoke-on-Trent, England. The original Bizooka was used by Clarice as an advertising display. *Photograph by kind permission of Josiah Wedgwood and Sons Ltd., owners of the registered trademarks of Clarice Cliff and Bizarre.*

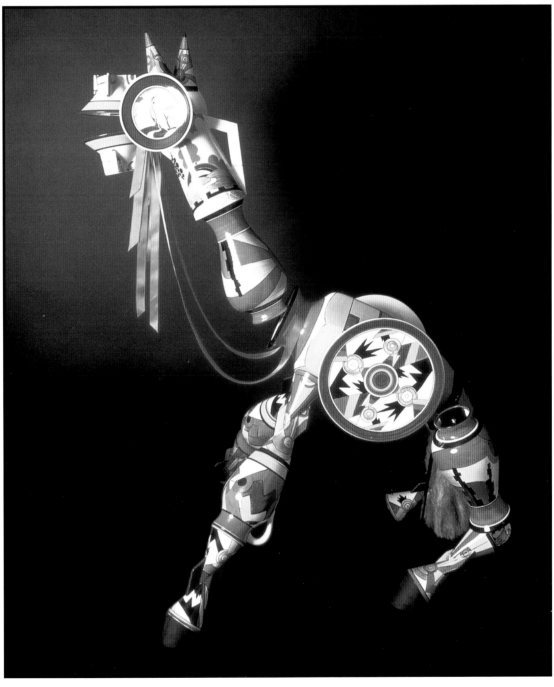

IDENTIFYING CLARICE CLIFF

To the initiated, the recognition of Clarice Cliff pottery soon becomes second nature. Many enthusiasts (including my children) can reel of hundreds of pattern names and identification is effortless.

To the new collector, identification is also generally no great problem, as the patterns and style are very recognisable. Generally, all Clarice Cliff pottery will have a backstamp, which both verifies pedigree and aids in dating. Many backstamps have the range or actual pattern name included. This information may also be hand painted above the backstamp. Together with the Clarice Cliff backstamp, you may also encounter the individual backstamp of the store where the piece was sold (e.g. Lawleys). Other marks to be found include pattern numbers and painters' marks. It is not unknown, however, for some pieces to leave the factory without a backstamp. In particular, many coffee cans and saucers only have a stamp on the saucer. Also, some items were too small to accommodate a backstamp (e.g. salt and pepper pots).

On flatware, e.g. plates and saucers, it is very common to find a small diamond impressed into the pottery, together with three numbers. This denotes the date of manufacture of the pottery, with the top number representing the month and the bottom numbers the year. Beware, however, that the piece could have been made many years prior to its decoration and, therefore, this only gives an approximation of the date it left the factory.

In addition to backstamps, items such as vases will have a shape number impressed on the underside. Generally, shape numbers were assigned chronologically and, therefore, the lower the number, the older the shape. However, many of the old shapes remained in production for many years. It is thought that shapes designed by Clarice Cliff start at 342, although shapes as early as number 200 do show signs of Art Deco influence and could be the work of Clarice Cliff.

Whereas the majority of patterns during the Bizarre era are now recorded, new patterns do continually emerge. It is also possible to find new variations of known patterns, e.g. different colored banding.

BACKSTAMPS

One of the Bizarre backstamps, used from the early to the mid-thirties.

The Biaritz mark and registration number relates to a Plate shape. When not accompanied by a Clarice Cliff backstamp, the designs are generally by Wilkinsons and probably not painted by the Bizarre girls.

Handwritten mark of the Inspiration range, c. 1929.

Many Bizarre backstamps include the name of the pattern. Originally it was handpainted; however, once the pattern became established the pattern name was included within the lithograph.

One of the backstamps for Fantasque, when it became integrated with the Bizarre range, c. 1931 to 1934.

Handwritten "Appliqué" mark together with Fantasque backstamp and the retailer's own backstamp, c. 1929.

Used from c. 1936 after Bizarre and Fantasque were phased out.

Unlike Clarice Cliff and Susie Cooper, Shelley is not the name of a designer, but is the name of the family firm of Shelley Potteries. In 1925, the Staffordshire pottery firm of Wileman & Co. (which by that time had become controlled by the Shelley family) changed its name to Shelley Potteries. Later, the firm became known as Shelley Potteries Ltd. Even so, the Shelley backstamp had been used by the company since 1910.

In terms of popularity, there are probably more collectors of Shelley than any other type of British pottery. One of the reasons for this is that Shelley products appeal to a much wider market than just Art Deco collectors.

As opposed to the earthenware pottery favoured by Clarice Cliff and Susie Cooper during the deco era, Shelley specialised in fine bone china in the main for their teaware (except for their Harmony range). The china was

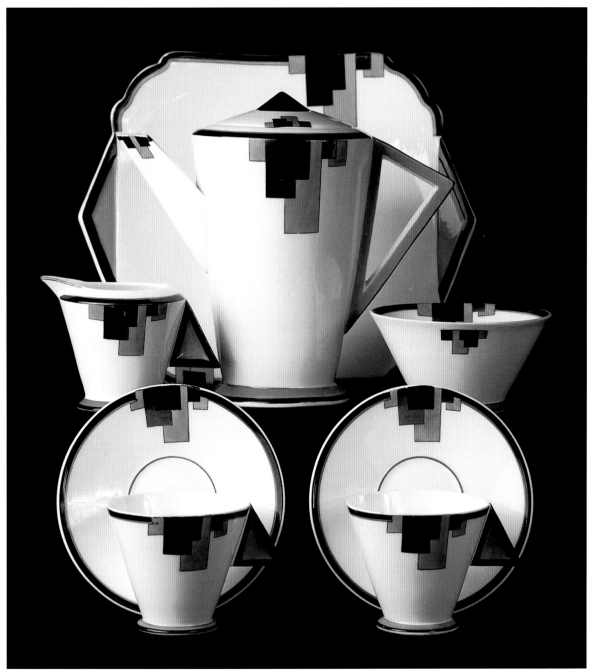

Shelley Vogue part Coffee Set in Green Geometric Blocks, Pattern No.11785. Bread and Butter Plate: $85, Coffeepot: $500, Milk and Sugar: $220, Individual Coffee Cans and Saucers: $250. *Courtesy of Decodance.*

produced to an exceptional standard and included a bone content as high as 52% (compared to a maximum today of 35%). This resulted in a finer and more translucent body for items such as cups. Greater translucency, together with the craftsmanship of the pieces, portrays a tremendous sense of quality to their products.

Shelley was also not slow to recognise the power of advertising and pursued vigourous advertising campaigns in the 1920/30s. They even took the somewhat unprecedented step of employing a professional advertising agency, called Smedley Services, and set aside large budgets unheard of for advertising. The agency created the "Shelley Girl" for advertising material, which featured a modern looking lady drinking tea from a Shelley cup. She was also modelled as a figurine, which is now very rare and keenly sought by collectors. As well as adverts in the leading magazines, the agency created lavish Retailers' color Catalogues

Designers of note at the factory were Frederick Rhead (up to 1905) and Walter Slater (up to 1928). They were both responsible for an Art Nouveau style of decoration called Intarsio. It is, however, Walter's son, Eric Slater, who is of most interest to Art Deco collectors.

Eric was trained at the Burslem and Hanley Schools of Art and worked for Shelley from 1919. He was, however, initially reluctant to join the Pottery industry and wanted to be an engineer for the Railways. Still, in 1928, he took over from his father as Art Director and Designer, completely changing the designs and direction of the firm. During his time with Shelley, Eric was responsible for introducing some of the most stylish of all products ever

A Shelley Queen Anne Coffeepot in the Trees and Sunset pattern. *Courtesy of Decodance.* $400.

Shelley part Tea Set in the Vogue shape and Coral Geometric Blocks pattern. Pattern No. 11786. Tea sets were not initially supplied with a teapot and the purchaser had the choice of adding the pot and that is why this set features a coffeepot. Trios: $375, Milk and Sugar: $300, Coffeepot: $500. *Courtesy of Decodance.*

produced by the British pottery industry. As I keep saying to anyone that will listen, "in terms of British Art Deco, Shelley is as good as it gets!"

The first major contribution by Eric was a series of patterns for the Queen Anne shape. This was a traditional shape introduced in 1926 that, in the main, featured floral and landscape patterns. Even though the shape was less daring than what was to follow, it included very distinctive octagonal cups and jugs. The range was immediately successful and continued to be produced for many years and included over 170 different patterns; the most famous patterns being Sunset and Tall Trees and Blue Iris.

The first real Art Deco shape that Eric introduced, in 1930, was the Vogue shape. This utilised traditional round saucers and the same shape desert plates as used for Queen Anne, but featured revolutionary shapes for the coffee pots, tea pots, milk jugs, coffee cans, and cups. The cups were of an extreme conical shape with solid triangular handles and these are the most prized possessions of Shelley Art Deco collectors. The Vogue cup, particularly in a pattern such as Sunray, is an icon of Deco design. The very fine bone china (approx 1mm thick), together with the shape, exude quality and decadence. A total of 53 different patterns are available on the Vogue shape, although some of these are color variants.

A very similar range introduced by Eric, also in 1930, was the Mode shape. Again, this features conical cups with solid triangular handles, although the conical shape is not as extreme as Vogue and the foot is not so pronounced. The majority of patterns on Vogue and Mode are geometric based, although stylised florals are to be found. The shape of coffee cans, milk jugs, tea and coffee pots and sugar bowls are common to both Vogue and Mode. On their introduction, *The Pottery Gazette* said "They may or may not carry the public by storm, but one thing they certainly will do, they will cause people to stop and think...There are those who for a long time past have been agitating for a more adventurous spirit in the manufacturing circles of the pottery trade. Well here it is!"

Despite the popularity with collectors, there were, at the time, many complaints from the public regarding the Vogue and Mode shaped cups. People complained that the handles were difficult to hold, they couldn't hang the cups on hooks, and that because of the wide surface area of the cups the liquid cooled too quickly.

In response to these complaints, Eric introduced the Eve shape in 1932. This is basically a Mode shape cup with an open triangular handle and a more definitive foot. The same geometric patterns used on Vogue and Mode were used on Eve; although, together with these, a multitude of floral patterns were also introduced. The design of Eve must have gone

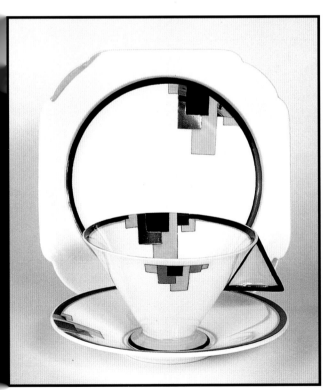

Shelley Trio in the Vogue shape with Yellow Geometric Blocks pattern. Pattern No. 11787. The design concept of the Vogue shape is very similar to the work of Grete Heymann-Marks, who was a member of the Bauhaus and later designer for the German Company of Haël-Werkstätten. *Courtesy of Decodance.* $350.

Vogue Tea Cup and Saucer in Blue Geometric Blocks, Pattern No. 11788. *Courtesy of Decodance.* $300.

a long way to address the complaints, as the shape continued in production until 1938, utilising 58 different patterns.

In 1932, Eric introduced the Regent shape. This was a departure from previous designs in that the cups lost their severe conical shape and angular handles. Instead, they featured open double rounded handles and trumpet shaped bodies. The shape was utilised for all forms of teaware and featured both geometric and floral patterns. Regent was very successful, using over 200 patterns and remaining in production well into the 1940s. The Regent shape was chosen by Gordon Forsyth as an item of good design and was featured in his book *20th Century Ceramics: an international survey of the best work*.

Alongside the bone china range, Eric also designed the Harmony dripware range. This was generally applied to earthenware and utilised a technique similar to Clarice Cliff's Delecia range. The paint was applied together with tur-

pentine and was allowed to freely flow down the pottery creating an effect similar to tie-dying. The technique was featured on all shapes of pottery, but is most effective on vases and chargers.

Shelley sold their tewares in sets and as individual items. Sets always excluded a teapot, an item that had to be bought separately. This is why some sets available today include a coffee pot as opposed to a teapot. Individual items were available to replace broken pieces, even after the pattern went out of production.

The company also found great success with a range of nurseryware for children. This featured designs by Hilda Cowham and Mabel Lucie Attwell. Both ladies were famous childrens' artists and illustrators. The work of Mabel Lucie Attwell is particularly collectible, including figurines, teapots shaped as ducks and toadstools, Boo Boo jugs in the shape of elves, and a mushroom sugar bowl.

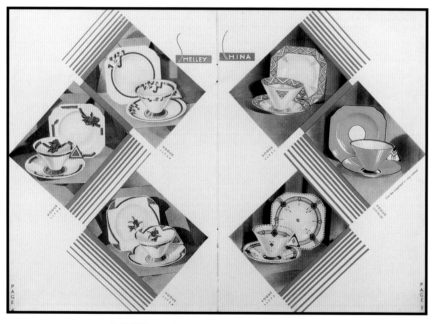

Extracts from the Shelley retail catalogue entitled "New Lines of Beauty From The House Of Shelley," which was produced by Smedley Advertising Services in 1929/30. The top photograph features a selection of Vogue trios and the bottom photograph, a selection of Mode trios. *Courtesy of Chris Davenport.*

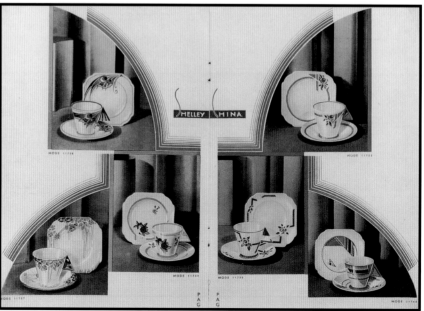

Left: A Shelley part Coffee Set in Blue Geometric Blocks, Pattern No. 11788. Coffeepot: $550, Milk and Sugar: $280, Individual Coffee Cans and Saucers: $300. *Courtesy of Decodance.*

Bottom: A selection of items in the Vogue shape and Sunray pattern, Pattern No.11742. Large Platter: $180, Trio (cup/saucer/ plate): $450, Coffeepot: $550, Bread and Butter Plate: $85, Coffee Can and Saucer: $250. *Courtesy of Decodance.*

A Shelley Vogue Coffeepot in the Sunray pattern. *Courtesy of Decodance.* $500.

Shelley Coffee Can and Saucer in Pattern No. 11743, one of the rarer alternative colorways of the Sunray pattern. *Courtesy of Decodance.* $300.

A Shelley six person Tea Set in the Vogue shape and Pattern No. 11776, featuring Chevron patterned handles. $3000 for the set. *Courtesy of M. Harland.*

Three Shelley Milk Jugs. Top: Eve shape with Gladioli pattern. Bottom: Vogue shape in Yellow Geometric Blocks and Butterfly. *Courtesy of Decodance.* $50-180.

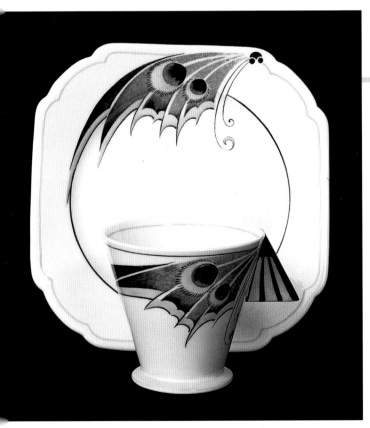

Shelley Cup and Plate in the Mode shape and Yellow Butterfly pattern. Pattern No. 11758. *Courtesy of Decodance.* Trio, $360.

Shelley Trio in the Eve shape and Gladiola pattern. Pattern No. 11961, c. 1932. *Courtesy of Decodance.* Trio, $150.

Shelley part Tea Set in Regent shape and Pattern No. WS 058. As well as the usual Shelley shield backstamp, these pieces are also marked "Ideal China" which is thought to be a special range for export to Canada. Trio: $70, Milk and Sugar: $70, Bread and Butter Plate: $75. *Courtesy of Decodance.*

Original Shelley label.

A Trio by Melba with a pattern and shape obviously influenced by Shelley. *Courtesy of Decodance.* $100

A group of Shelley Blue Harmony Dripware. *Photograph Courtesy of Bona Arts Decorative Ltd.* $45-100.

A group of Shelley Orange Harmony Dripware. *Photograph Courtesy of Bona Arts Decorative Ltd.* $45-150.

Various items in
Shelley Blue Harmony
Dripware. *Courtesy of
Decodance.* $30-120.

Shelley Harmony
Dripware. *Courtesy of
Decodance.* $30-100.

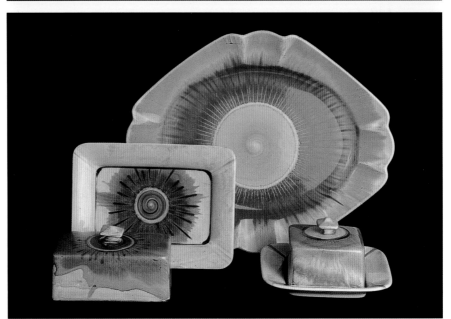

A selection of Shelley
Harmony Dripware.
*Courtesy of
Decodance.* $60-80.

A selection of figures designed for Shelley by Mabel Lucie Attwell. *Courtesy of Banana Dance*. NP

IDENTIFYING SHELLEY

With the exception of some Harmony pieces, most Shelley items have three marks on the underneath. They have a pattern number, a registration number, and a backstamp. These marks can be very useful in dating and identifying pieces, e.g. particularly when telephoning auction houses to ascertain exactly what they have.

Pattern Numbers

Pattern numbers used in the deco era, generally consist of a five figure number. The patterns were given numbers in chronological order and can help date a piece. Set out below is a list of the first pattern numbers for each particular year

Pattern Number	First introduced:
11458	1926
11539	1927
11600	1928
11648	1929
11717	1930
11818	1931
11936	1932
12115	1933
12267	1934
12361	1935
12450	1936
12589	1937
12683	1938
12882	1939

Pattern numbers for Queen Anne start at 11475 and end at 12202.
Pattern numbers for Vogue start at 11738 and end at 12136.
Pattern numbers for Mode start at 11755 and end at 11871.
Pattern numbers for Eve start at 11950 and end at 12992.

Registration Numbers

Together with the pattern number, a further number is to be found that represents the copyright of the shape. This number is preceded by the letters Rd. The following are of interest to Art Deco collectors.

723404	Queen Anne
756533	Vogue and Mode
781613	Regent

BACKSTAMPS

Shelley backstamp in black, used from 1925 to 1945.

Shelley backstamp in green, used from 1925 to 1945.

Shelley backstamp used only on china, from 1930 to 1932.

Chapter 7

THE SUPPORTING CAST

BARKER BROTHERS

The company of Barker Brothers (1876-1959) produced many floral, geometric, and landscape patterns on all kinds of teaware. However, the most collectible patterns produced by Barker Brothers are those designed by John Guildford. He joined the firm in 1922, after leaving his employment with Grays, were he worked for a short time with Susie Cooper. Some examples of Guildford's designs have a backstamp that includes his name, giving him the distinction of being one of the few males to have a "designer label."

It is alleged that John Guildford taught Clarice Cliff when she attended the Burslem School of Art. Indeed, there are some noticeable similarities between their work. John Guildford has a range of patterns called "Arabesque" and Clarice Cliff has a range called "Fantasque." John Guildford has a pattern called "The Garden" and Clarice Cliff has a pattern called "My Garden." Even the backstamps of the two designers are reminiscent of each other, using similar layout and script.

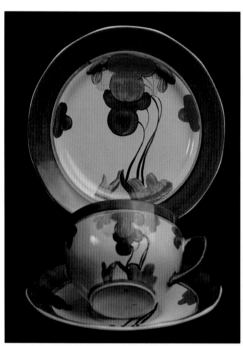

Trio by John Guildford. *Courtesy of Decodance.* $120.

Barker Brothers backstamp.

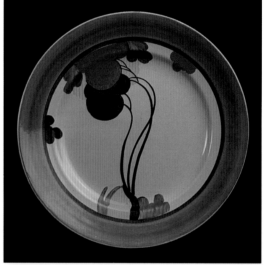

Left: Plate designed by John Guildford for Barker Brothers. Displaying a similarity to the Clarice Cliff Autumn pattern. *Courtesy of Decodance.* $120.

Below: Two Plates by John Guildford in the Arabesque pattern. *Courtesy of Decodance.* $50 each.

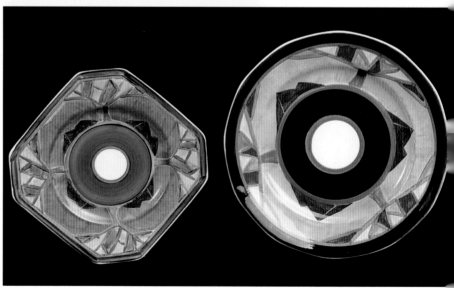

BESWICK

The firm of John Beswick Ltd. (1890-1964) is perhaps better known for its range of decorative items, including a series of Beatrix Potter animal figures. They also produced a range of tableware called "Sundial" that purported to be Art Deco. It was a hideous amalgamation of Aztec stepped handles with quant English garden scenes in pinks and browns, and lids in sundial shapes.

However, they also produced a selection of Art Deco jugs and face masks, the latter being of greatest interest to Art Deco collectors. The most sought after of the masks is an example modelled on Marlene Dietrich. This is available in different colorways including variations to hair and bonnet colors.

The firm also produced that icon of kitsch, the graduated set of wall hangings in the shape of flying ducks, which have graced many a Monty Python set. These were extremely popular and were produced in sets of Mallards, Kingfishers, Swallows, and Seagulls.

The usual pre-war backstamp uses the words "Beswick Ware" in script, with the words "Made in England" below in capitals. The post-war backstamp reads "Beswick England".

The Beatrix Potter figures, and a series of figures depicting Snow White and the seven dwarfs, demand the greatest prices. Wall masks are becoming relatively expensive in view of their popularity, starting at approximately $350. Although, jugs are quite affordable and can be obtained for as little as $75.

A large Wall Mask by Beswick. 12 inches high. *Courtesy of Decodance.* $500.

Wall Mask by Beswick, mod-elled on Marlene Dietrich. *Courtesy of Decodance.* $450.

Beswick Vase with original label. *Courtesy of Decodance.* $75.

Beswick Flower Jug. *Courtesy of Decodance.* $120.

BURLEIGH WARE

Dating back to the 1850s, the firm of Burgess and Leigh is still in existence today. They have produced pottery for over a hundred years at the same factory at Middleport, Burslem, in the Potteries. The brand name for their pottery is Burleigh Ware.

In the 1920s, Burgess and Leigh switched the emphasis from toilet and general earthenware to the production of tea and dinnerware. The company introduced its own shapes, including Sheraton (1930), Zenith (1931), and London (1932).

The most popular shape with Art Deco collectors is the Zenith shape, which was modelled by the companies own in house designer, Edward Bailey. The Zenith shape is a combination of straight lines and curves in a conical form that is not extreme. It could be described as a typical English adaptation of Art Deco. In sympathy with the shape, the patterns were also rather "safe" in an English way.

The patterns applied to the shapes, including Pan, Dawn, Meadowland, and Moonbeams, were also designed in house by art director, Harold Bennett.

The rarest and most collectible of the Burleigh Ware Jugs is the 8 inch Guards Jug. Issued in 1933, it was available in two variations. The one shown here has the soldiers marching around the jug. It was also available in various colorways including soldiers with black trousers and orange stripe, green trousers with black stripe, and yellow trousers with black stripe. *Photograph by and Courtesy of Elizabeth Coupe.* $3000+.

Commonly found on many Burleigh Ware patterns are painted black dots on the edges of the pieces. This feature was also a technique used by the firm of Crown Ducal.

Burleigh Ware tea and dinnerware is currently fairly plentiful and (for the time being) available at modest prices. Together with teaware, the company also produced a range of jugs (pitchers). These, like the teaware, were modelled by Ernest Bailey, with patterns designed by Harold Bennett. However, these jugs can command very high prices. A common feature of the jugs is the specialised deep yellow glaze of the body. The patterns followed various themes including birds and animals, and, generally, the handle of the jug was modelled to reflect the theme.

One of the most popular series of the jugs is the "Sportsmen" range, which was issued as a "Cricketer," "Golfer," and "Tennis Player." The company also produced some highly stylized Deco shapes including Loz-

A Burleigh Ware Teapot in the Zenith shape and Pan pattern. *Photograph by and Courtesy of Elizabeth Coupe.* $175.

Above: A Burleigh Ware Coffeepot in the Zenith shape and Meadowland pattern. *Photograph by and Courtesy of Elizabeth Coupe.* $100.

Left: A Burleigh Ware Guards Jug, c. 1933. The second variation features a sentry box with a soldier on the back and front. *Photograph by and Courtesy of Elizabeth Coupe.* $3000+.

enge Jugs, Totem Jugs, and Double Diamond Vases.

By far, the most desirable of Burleigh Ware pieces is their "Guardsman Jug." Unlike the majority of the jugs, this was not popular at its time of issue and was, therefore, not made in the same quantities as other jugs. Consequently, it is now very rare and, even if you can find one, it will cost somewhere in the region of $4500.

Charlotte Rhead was employed by the firm as a designer from 1926 to 1931. During her time there, she designed many pieces depicting stylised florals and landscapes together with wall plaques featuring Galleons and seascapes in the Art Deco style.

Generally, all Burleigh Ware items are marked with a backstamp; some pieces will have the pattern printed on the underside. The general pre-war backstamp is a beehive surrounded by foilage. After the war, the beehive was smaller with no foilage.

Part of the Burleigh Ware Sportsman series, the Cricketer Jug was issued in 1935. 8 inches high. *Photograph by and Courtesy of Elizabeth Coupe.* $1000+.

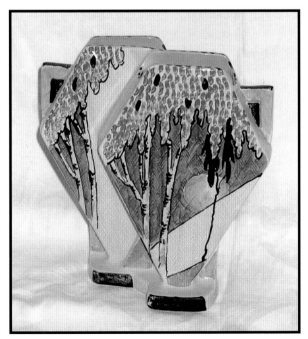

Above: The Golfer Jug was the first Burleigh Ware Sportsman Jug, issued in 1934. Others included in the series were the Criketer and the Tennis Player. *Photograph by and Courtesy of Elizabeth Coupe.* $1000+.

Left: Double Lozenge Vase by Burleigh Ware. *Photograph by and courtesy of Elizabeth Coupe.* $800.

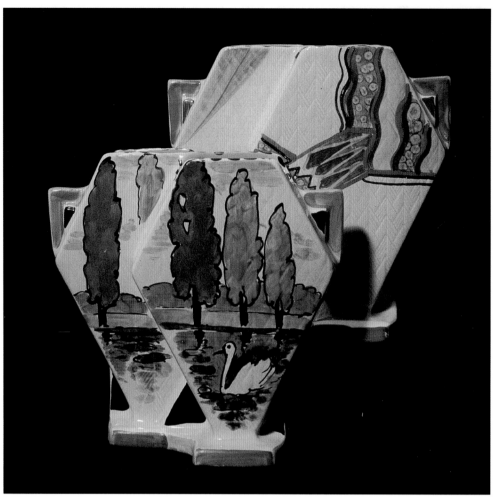

Two Double Lozenge Jugs by Burleigh. *Photograph Courtesy of Bona Arts Decorative Ltd.* $800 each.

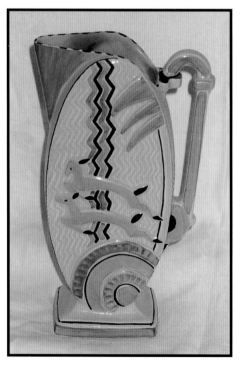

Leaping Gazelle Jug by Burleigh Ware. *Photograph by and courtesy of Elizabeth Coupe.* $600.

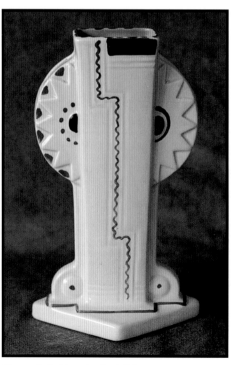

Totem Pole Vase by Burleigh Ware. *Photograph by and Courtesy of Elizabeth Coupe.* $600.

Lozenge shaped Galleon Jug by Burleigh Ware, available in different colorways including a red ship with green sea and black ship with yellow sea. *Photograph by and Courtesy of Elizabeth Coupe.* $650.

CARLTON WARE

Of all the pottery featured in this chapter, Carlton Ware is perhaps the most collectible. The range certainly deserves greater coverage than space permits in this book. However, one of the reasons why I have chosen to limit such coverage is that the reader has the opportunity to delve further via books dedicated to the pottery.

Carlton Ware enjoys great popularity with collectors and has been subject to noticeable increases in value over the last few years. The key factor for the success of Carlton Ware, both at the time of its production and now, is its sheer quality. The firm specialised in innovative lustre finishes combined with complex transfer printing and hand-painting techniques.

Unlike many other pottery firms, they did not market their wares under the name of the designers. Instead, they preferred to rely on their brand name, Carlton Ware. The wares were originally produced by the firm of Wiltshaw and Robinson (established in 1890), who produced the pottery at the Carlton Works, Stoke-on-Trent, in the Pottereies. Up to 1927, the backstamp of Carlton Ware included the initials of the company. In 1925, a new backstamp was introduced alongside the original that excluded the initials and featured Carlton Ware written in script.

Vase in the Rosetta pattern. *Photograph by and courtesy of CWCI & St Clare-Carlton Ware.* $150-450.

Vase in the classic deco pattern, Jazz. *Photograph by and courtesy of CWCI & St Clare-Carlton Ware.* $450-750.

Vase in the Geometric pattern. *Photograph by and courtesy of CWCI & St Clare-Carlton Ware.* $1500-2000.

The discovery of the tomb of Tutankhamen in Egypt in 1922 was one of the major influences on Art Deco. Carlton Ware responded to this by introducing designs featuring Egyptian motifs and hieroglyphs.

After the 1925 Paris exhibition, designers generally became more liberated and Carlton Ware followed this trend. They continued to issue patterns drawing on Egyptian influences, but extended their ranges to include Fantasy designs to compete with Wedgwoods "Fairy Lustre" range. This included such patterns as Fantasia, Fairy and Red Devil.

By 1930, Carlton Ware was reaching an artistic peak. The decade saw some of their most adventurous and desirable pieces. Both geometrics and highly stylized patterns utilizing lightning flashes, sunbursts, and explosions were combined with their superlative lustre techniques. Particularly memorable patterns of this era included Spangled Tree, Rainbow Fan, Jazz, Deco Fan, Intersections, Lightning, Zig Zag, Scimitar, Mondrian, and Geometrica.

In 1929, the company introduced a range called Handcraft. As the name suggests, this featured freehand designs. The range did not utilise the expensive lustre process and relied on a matt glaze with softer colors, although it was available in high glaze or a combination of glazes. Generally, each piece has the word "Handcraft" incorporated into the script mark. The range was sold at much cheaper prices than the lustrewares; however, Handcraft pieces today demand high prices due to the limited production.

After the Second World War, Carlton Ware continued to produce new lustre ranges and gained recognition for its Guinness advertising ware. The factory continued until 1989, having been purchased by Wood and Co. in 1967. Carlton Ware was relaunched in 1990 by Grosvenor Ceramics and was subsequently sold to Francis Joseph Publications in 1997, who are reintroducing Carlton Ware items back on the market.

Bowl in Stellata. *Photograph by and courtesy of CWCI & St Clare-Carlton Ware.* $750-1000.

Above: Vase in Hiawatha pattern. *Photograph by and courtesy of CWCI & St Clare- Carlton Ware.* $250+.

Right: Part Coffee Set in the Geometric Butterfly pattern. *Photograph by and courtesy of CWCI & St Clare-Carlton Ware.* $750-1200.

Vase with the Anemone pattern. *Photograph by and courtesy of CWCI & St Clare-Carlton Ware.* $3000+.

Pitcher in Chevrons. *Photograph by and courtesy of CWCI & St Clare-Carlton Ware.* $750-1000.

The Red Devil pattern shown on a Biscuit Barrel and Pitcher. *Courtesy of a member of CWCI.* $3000+ each.

Bookends in Flower Fan. *Photograph by and courtesy of CWCI & St Clare-Carlton Ware.* $200+.

Dear Napkin Ring. *Photograph by and courtesy of CWCI & St Clare-Carlton Ware.* $75-125.

Above: Powder Bowl in the Fan pattern with Figurehead Handle. *Photograph by and courtesy of CWCI & St Clare-Carlton Ware.* $750+.

Right: Profile detail of the Figurehead Handle. *Photograph by and courtesy of CWCI & St Clare- Carlton Ware.*

A Wall Plate in the
Russian pattern.
*Photograph by and
courtesy of CWCI &
St Clare-Carlton
Ware.* $3000+.

Above: Jazz Stitch pattern on a Revo Dish.
*Photograph by and courtesy of CWCI & St
Clare-Carlton Ware.* $250+.

Left: Ginger Jar in the Devil's Copse pattern.
*Photograph by and courtesy of CWCI & St
Clare-Carlton Ware.* $1000-1500.

The Waggon Wheels pattern on a Vase.
*Photograph by and courtesy of CWCI &
St Clare-Carlton Ware.* $750-1200.

A modernist type Coffee Can and Saucer by
Carlton Ware. *Courtesy of Decodance.* $100.

Tea for Two in the Rayure pattern on the Modern shape. *Photograph
by and courtesy of CWCI & St Clare-Carlton Ware.* $1500+.

Coffee Set by Carlton Ware.
Courtesy of Decodance. $700.

Vase in unknown pattern. *Photograph by and courtesy of CWCI & St Clare- Carlton Ware.* $150+.

Vase showing the Orchid pattern.
Photograph by and courtesy of CWCI & St Clare-Carlton Ware. $750+.

Vase and a pair of Candlesticks in the Fan pattern. *Photograph by and courtesy of CWCI & St Clare-Carlton Ware.* $750-3000.

Above right: The Secretary Bird and Scimitar patterns. *Photograph by and courtesy of CWCI & St Clare-Carlton Ware.* $1500-3000.

Above: Vase in the Carnival pattern. *Photograph by and courtesy of CWCI & St Clare-Carlton Ware.* $750-1000.

Right: Pitcher with the Awakening pattern. *Photograph by and courtesy of CWCI & St Clare-Carlton Ware.* $3000 +.

Identifying Carlton Ware

There are generally three possible clues to identifying and dating Carlton Ware: pattern numbers, shape numbers and backstamps. Pattern numbers were generally hand painted onto the base of each piece. Carlton's main earthenware range issued numbers supposedly from 1 through to at least 6000, although no records exist to corroborate this. Confusion arises during the 1930s, when bone china was produced. These pieces have the same pattern numbers as many of the earthenware ranges. Very approximately, pattern numbers up to 3000 predate 1930 and up to 4300 predate 1940.

Some pieces also have a shape number. This is a number that is impressed into the clay during the moulding stage. It obviously identifies the shape, but it can also assist in dating. Although, be aware that the shape number does not provide accurate dating, as a shape could well have been used for many years after its first date of production. Like pattern numbers, shape numbers were introduced consecutively and set out below are the approximate dates when shape numbers were first introduced.

SHAPE NUMBER	FIRST INTRODUCED
1000	1934
1200	1935
1400	1936
1500	1937
1600	1938
1700	1939
1800	1940

Vase in the cubist influenced Mondrian pattern. *Photograph by and courtesy of CWCI & St Clare-Carlton Ware.* $850-1000.

Temple Jar in the Zig Zag pattern. *Photograph by and courtesy of CWCI & St Clare-Carlton Ware.* $3000+.

Dish in the Geometric Sunflower pattern. *Photograph by and courtesy of CWCI & St Clare-Carlton Ware.* $750.

CHAMELEON WARE

Chameleon Ware was manufactured by the firm of George Clews & Co. Ltd., from the early 1900s to 1961. The firm produced a number of items including plain glazes with incised patterns, floral patterns, some patterns that were very similar to Poole, and a range of Rock Garden Ornaments. However, they are generally best known today for their distinctive "Flame" patterns. Flame patterns exhibit an Egyptian influence and were produced in Green, Brown, Cream and, most commonly, Blue variations.

The company also produced, under licence, the Cube Teapot, which was used as Hotel Ware and on the Cunard Ocean liners. The trademark used by the company during the 1930s was, aptly, a Chameleon within a triangle and this is generally used as a backstamp on their pottery. Other marks on such items as vases include an impressed number to denote the shape and a painted number that refers to the pattern.

Chameleon Ware by George Clewes & Co. Ltd. *Photograph by and courtesy of Hilary Calvert.* $75-250.

Chameleon Ware together with a ceramic lizard, after which the wares are named. *Photograph by and courtesy of Hilary Calvert.* $75-200.

Chameleon Ware with various colorways of the Flame design.
Photograph by and courtesy of Hilary Calvert. $100-225

Various Pitchers in Chameleon Ware. *Photograph
by and courtesy of Hilary Calvert.* $150-250.

Charger by Charlotte Rhead. *Courtesy of Banana Dance.* NP

Charger by Wood & Son, marked No. 1876, 41 cm
wide. *Courtesy of Banana Dance.* NP

CHARLOTTE RHEAD

Born in 1885, Charlotte Rhead was the daughter of the famous art designer, Frederick Rhead. Her brother, also called Frederick, became a designer for the Roseville Pottery in the USA.

Throughout her career, Charlotte Rhead designed for various factories, many of which were in conjunction with her father. Some of her designs are more akin to Art Nouveau, and she specialised in " tube-lining." This is a process similar to icing a cake, where the pattern is outlined by a thin line of clay, applied to the body of the pottery.

In approximately 1913, she joined her father at Wood & Sons, where he was Art Director, and produced designs labeled Lottie Rhead Ware. From 1926, she designed for Burgess and Leigh (see Burleigh Ware) and left that company in 1931 to work for A.G. Richardson.

There she produced many designs under the Crown Ducal trademark. The majority of shapes she used were traditional and included vases, jugs and an enormous array of plaques and chargers. Patterns for Crown Ducal included Stitch, Persian Rose, Golden Leaves, Byzantine, and Aztec. Most of her Crown Ducal designs have a Charlotte Rhead backstamp and some pieces have her name tube lined as part of the backstamp.

In 1942, she returned to work for Wood & Sons as a designer for their subsidiary company, H.J. Wood Ltd. Her designs were generally issued as part of their Bursley Ware range. She remained with the company, until she died in 1947.

Crown Ducal Wallpocket in the Byzantine pattern, which can also be used as a freestanding Vase. Signed Charlotte Rhead and marked 143 and 2681. *Courtesy of Jane Fryer.* $450.

Charger designed by Charlotte Rhead for Crown Ducal. Marked 6189. *Courtesy of Jane Fryer.* $450.

Twin handled Vase painted with primula flowers. Designed by Charlotte Rhead for Crown Ducal. $500.

Above left: Vase in the Byzantine pattern by Charlotte Rhead for Crown Ducal. $450

Above right: Vase by Charlotte Rhead in the Rhodian pattern for Crown Ducal. Marked 176 and 3272. *Courtesy of D & P Hawkins.* $500.

Left: Crown Ducal Ewer. Marked 146 and 5983. Not signed. *Courtesy of D & P Hawkins.* $400.

Below: Ashtray by Frederick Rhead in the Chung pattern. *Courtesy of Decodance.* $95.

COPES & CO.

Although the firm of J.H. Cope & Co. Ltd. produced teaware for over sixty years, they are better known now for their range of face masks. These masks featured stylized young ladies with a definite continental look. Very often they were depicted with beads and headware. The range includes full face and profile (generally facing to the left) masks. They were made in various sizes and different colorways can be found.

Generally, the masks have the initials "C & Co" impressed on the back. Still, it is quite common to find examples with no distinguishing factory marks.

Wall Mask by Copes and Co. *Courtesy of Decodance.* $180.

CROWN DEVON

The firm of Fielding & Co., owned by the Fielding family, produced pottery from the 1870s to the 1980s. Their products were generally issued under the Crown Devon trade name. The range and output issued over a period in excess of 100 years was massive and varied. Many Crown Devon designs bear a close resemblance to other potteries. Their lustrewares are similar to Carlton Ware, a fact that is, perhaps, explained by the defection of Carlton Ware designers Enoch Wood and George Baker to the Crown Devon factory in 1930. Also, a range of Cubist geometrics issued by the company are very reminiscent of the early designs produced by Susie Cooper for A.E. Grays.

In the mid-1930s, Fielding & Co. introduced a range of very striking coffee sets. Some of these utilised the Moderne shape with sophisticated patterns incorporating zigzags and lightning flashes. The quality of these sets is exceptional and very often includes lustre interiors. The sets were sometimes sold with trays or in luxurious boxes. As noted by Judy Spours, "in these bold designs, there is no indication that Crown Devon were looking for an Anglicized style: their interpretation of Art Deco is exotic." [1]

The company also produced an extensive range of table lamps and figurines, many of which were modelled by Kathleen Parsons. The usual backstamp is a Crown with the words "Crown Devon" underneath on two lines.

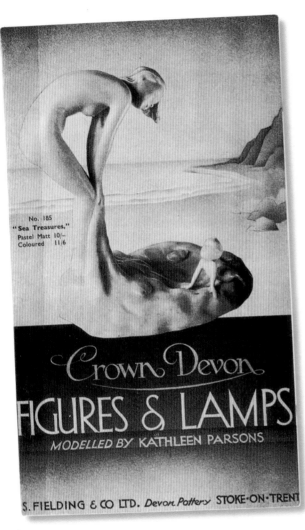

No. 185
"Sea Treasures."
Pastel Matt 10/–
Coloured   11/6

Crown Devon
FIGURES & LAMPS
MODELLED BY KATHLEEN PARSONS

S. FIELDING & CO LTD. *Devon Pottery* STOKE·ON·TRENT

Right: An elegent Hollywood Style figurine, "The Beach Girl" by Crown Devon. *Courtesy of Banana Dance.* $4000+.

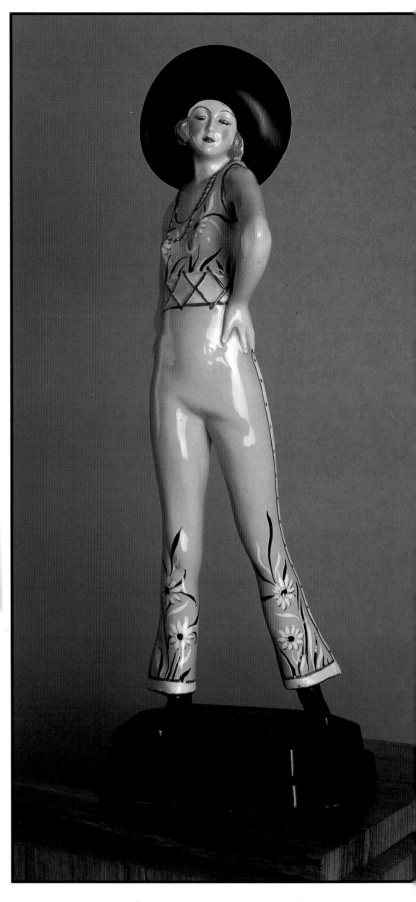

Left: Part Coffee Set by Crown Devon. *Courtesy of Decodance.* $225.

Lower left: Crown Devon figurine "Fairy Secrets," No. 186, modelled by Kathleen Parsons for Crown Devon. *Courtesy of Banana Dance.* NP

Lower right: Crown Devon figurine, "Autumn Leaves," modelled by Kathleen Parsons. *Courtesy of Banana Dance.* NP

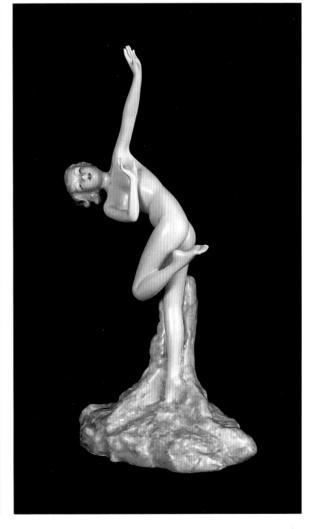

Crown Devon Coffee
Can and Saucer,
marked A71. *Courtesy
of Decodance.* $150.

Crown Devon Coffee Can and Saucer.
The Geometric pattern is very similar to
the early designs by Susie Cooper for
Grays. *Courtesy of Decodance.* $230.

A part Coffee Set by Crown Devon in Mattajade.
Photograph Courtesy of Bona Arts Decorative Ltd. NP

Crown Devon
backstamp.

KEITH MURRAY

Keith Murray was born in New Zealand in 1892 and later moved to Britain. He was an active member of the Royal Flying Corps during World War One, and was awarded the Military Cross. Trained as an architect, his approach to design was minimalist; he concentrated on form rather than decoration.

Murray worked as a design consultant for numerous companies. He designed glass for Stevens and Williams and luxury metalwork items for Mappin and Webb. In 1933, he was commissioned by the major Staffordshire pottery company of Josiah Wedgwood and Sons, to produce ceramic designs. As stated by Judy Spours, "Murray immediately came to grips with the important issue of modern shapes as opposed to new decorations. The vast majority of his ceramic designs were for simple, Modernist, architectural shapes, which were decorated in a variety of plain colored glazes developed by Norman Smith. Here at last was an industrial ceramic designer who concentrated on form rather than decoration, and who designed shapes which were simple, modern, yet thoroughly English, containing echoes of traditional Wedgwood classical shapes."[2]

Publicity material at the time claimed, "he has seen how to build on the Wedgwood tradition an entirely new style of design, making full use of Wedgwood craftsmanship and fineness of material. His designs are characterised by virile shapes and clear cut outline, and are, in the large majority of cases, executed by the traditional methods of Throwing and Turning, in which Wedgwood craftsmen excel."

Murray's first project with Wedgwood was to assist with their Anular shaped teaware. Later, he designed a coffee set comprised of a tall coffee pot with a stepped lid and straight sided coffee cans, devoid of any decoration except a series of turned grooves (although, it was available with platinum colored handles).

The coffee set, like the majority of Keith Murray designs, relied heavily on specially developed glazes, which included the semi matt

Keith Murray with a "Commonwealth" shape teapot, c. 1946. *Photograph courtesy of the Trustees of The Wedgwood Museum, Barleston, Staffordshire, England.*

Moonstone and less typically Celadon Satin. Other items designed for Wedgwood include vases, bowls, ashtrays, book-ends, wall pockets, pen and ink stands, candlesticks, and cigarette boxes.

Keith Murray ceramic designs are generally instantly recognisable. They successfully combine form with function and any decoration accentuates the form. Due to their enormous success at the time of pro-duction, examples today are quite widely available.

Prices, however, have tended to rise steeply over the past few years. Although, if you are on a limited budget, you can still obtain one of the classic Keith Murray beer mugs for a small outlay. The beer mugs were designed in 1934 and issued in various colors including Moonstone, straw, and green. Wedgwood's promotional literature sug-

A selection of pieces by Keith Murray. *Photograph by and Courtesy of Carole A Berk Ltd.* $150-3000 +.

gested that "apart from their good looks, they have other advantages... they are particularly pleasant to drink from, because of their smooth surface, and they have a positive gift for making good beer taste even better."

Whereas fakes of Keith Murray have yet to emerge, a number of other pottery companies in the 1930s, including Sylvac, tried to copy his designs and glazes. These, however, are generally clearly marked.

Usually, all Keith Murray pieces are marked with a backstamp. The pre-1941 backstamp includes "Keith Murray" written in script in full, whilst the backstamp used after 1941 only includes the initials "KM".

Keith Murray, also contributed to the success of Wedgwood in other ways; he designed their new factory at Barlaston, near Stoke-on-Trent, in 1938.

Coffee Set and various Vases by Keith Murray. *Photograph by and Courtesy of Carole A Berk Ltd.* $500-2000+.

Vases by Keith Murray. *Courtesy of Decodance.* $600 each.

Beer Mug by Keith Murray. Pre-war backstamp, 4.75 inches high. It was available in numerous colors. *Courtesy of Decodance.* $120.

Annular Vase designed by Keith Murray. Earthenware with a matt-green glaze. *Courtesy of Decodance.* $600.

Above: Advertisement featuring an Annular Vase, c. 1936. *Photograph courtesy of the Trustees of The Wedgwood Museum, Barleston, Staffordshire, England.*

Right: Extract from Wedgwood factory records, featuring outline drawings of Keith Murray designs, dated October 1939. *Photograph courtesy of the Trustees of The Wedgwood Museum, Barleston, Staffordshire, England.*

Below: Keith Murray pre-war backstamp.

Keith Murray
WEDGWOOD
MADE N ENGLAND

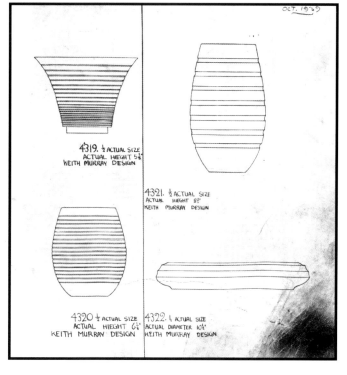

OCT. 1939

4319. ½ ACTUAL SIZE
ACTUAL HIEGHT 5⅛"
KEITH MURRAY DESIGN

4321. ½ ACTUAL SIZE
ACTUAL HIEGHT 8⅛"
KEITH MURRAY DESIGN

4320 ½ ACTUAL SIZE
ACTUAL HIEGHT 6⅛"
KEITH MURRAY DESIGN

4322. ¼ ACTUAL SIZE
ACTUAL DIAMETER 10⅛"
KEITH MURRAY DESIGN

LOUIS WAIN

Louis Wain is best known for his drawings of cats. In the early 1900s, he was a household name and his drawings were featured on postcards and in many books. He became obsessed with cats and was committed to the Middlesex County Asylum. There he spent the remainder of his days until he died in 1939. During his time at the asylum, his drawings changed from his usual trademark of cute playful kittens to "schizophrenic art." These, today, are used by psychiatrists to illustrate the stages of mental illness.

Of interest to Art Deco collectors are a series of ceramic animal figures based on his designs. The figures are heavily influenced by cubism and exhibit a distinctive psychotic style. The series includes many cats (some of which look more like dogs), lions, pigs, and even robots. They were brightly hand painted and were adorned with numerous strange hieroglyphics, including Wain's "Meow Meow" notes.

They are usually signed by Louis Wain and some have apertures at the back to enable them to be used as small vases. Many of the figures were given names; the robot was called "The Knight Errant" and the most frequently found cat was called "The Lucky Haw Haw Cat."

A more conventional cat figure was also designed by Louis Wain for the pottery firm of Wilkinsons. A version of this figure, called "The Laughing Cat," was issued by Clarice Cliff as part of her Bizarre range.

Above: Pig by Louis Wain. *Courtesy of Decodance.* $1500.

Left: Black Cat. Spill Vase by Louis Wain. *Courtesy of Banana Dance.* NP

The Lucky Haw-Haw Cat by Louis Wain. A Spill Vase,
5.75 inches high. *Courtesy of Banana Dance*. NP

Felix the Futurist Cat by Louis Wain, 9.5 inches
high. *Courtesy of Banana Dance*. NP

Cat Vase by Louis Wain. *Courtesy of Banana Dance*. NP

Bulldog by Louis Wain. *Courtesy of Banana Dance*. NP

The Lucky Knight Errant Cat by Louis Wain. A Spill Vase, 5.75 inches high. Highlighted with black meow-meow notes. *Courtesy of Banana Dance*. NP

The Lion Cat by Louis Wain. *Courtesy of Banana Dance*. NP

MYOTT

Myott and Son did not utilise any trade name or designer label. Instead, they merely issued their products under the name of the company. They were established in the late 1800s and operated from the Alexander Pottery in the Potteries from 1925.

Their products are wide ranging, from simple floral teaware to extreme Art Deco shaped vases and jugs. Although some of the vases and jugs are crudely painted, they are highly desirable for their shapes.

The most collectible vases are the Pyramid, the Fan, the Bowtie, the Torpedo, and the Castle vase. The range of jugs (pitchers) is quite extensive and includes a multitude of shapes. These range from the mundane to the sublime. The most commonly found jug (and the least desirable) is the "Pinch Jug," and the rarest are the Bowtie and the very rare Beaky jugs (sometimes called the Penguin).

Collectors may also encounter Face Masks and Figurines in the style of the Austrian firm of Goldschieder. These are marked "Goldschieder (Myott)", which suggests that Myott may have produced some of the Goldschieder range under license in England.

Decoration for the pottery included Czechoslovakian peasant type florals, rather muted earthy browns, colourful wash-banding, and very bold and vivid geometrics.

The usual backstamp of the factory is a gold crown with the words " Myott Son & Co" and "Hand painted. Made in England" underneath. Various pattern numbers, are also printed on the pottery; however, the Pattern Books and the records of the company are no longer available, having been destroyed in a fire at the factory.

A selection of pieces by Myott including a Pyramid, Castle and Fan Vase. *Photograph Courtesy of Bona Arts Decorative Ltd.* $60-400.

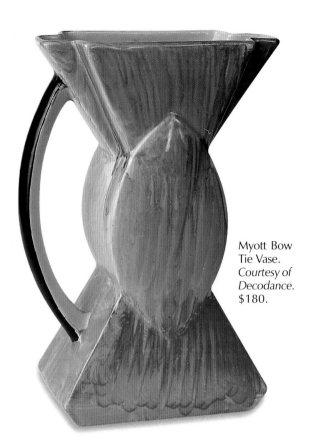

Myott Bow Tie Vase. *Courtesy of Decodance.* $180.

Myott Pyramid Vase. *Courtesy of Decodance.* $250.

An extremely colorful Bow Tie Jug by Myott, c. 1934. *Courtesy of Jean May.* $500.

POOLE

One of the few pottery companies operating outside the Potteries, the firm of Carter and Co. was established at Poole in Dorset in 1873. The firm was joined by Harold Stabler in 1913 and John and Truda Adams in 1921. From that date, the company was known as Carter, Stabler and Adams. Although, their wares were generally referred to as Poole Pottery, and the company eventually changed its name to Poole Pottery Ltd. in 1963.

The company was highly successful at combining art and commercial pottery. They specialised in naturalistic designs featuring stylized flora on a silky matt glaze. A frequent motif to be found within the designs is the Leaping Deer. Famous designers working at the factory included Truda Carter and Phoebe Stabler. Prominent paintresses included Ann Hatchand and Ruth Pavely.

The designs of the 1920s and '30s are now very collectible and offer an element of tranquility from the more strident designs usually associated with the era.

Various marks are to be found on Poole Pottery including factory marks, pattern codes (generally two letters), shape numbers, and painter's marks.

Above: Vase by Carter, Stabler and Adams, ZB pattern code. *Courtesy of Banana Dance.* $750+.

Left A Vase by Carter, Stabler and Adams in Persian Deer. Pattern code SK. *Courtesy of Banana Dance.* $750+.

Vase by Carter, Stabler and Adams. EP pattern
code. *Courtesy of Banana Dance*. $1000+.

Poole Pitcher in Shape 315.
Courtesy of Banana Dance. $450.

Bowl by Poole. Pattern code ED. The pattern is often
wrongly called Fuschia. *Courtesy of Decodance*. $200.

Honeybox by Carter, Stabler and Adams. The example
features a bee finial, but it was also available with others
including a pelican finial. *Courtesy of Decodance*. $350.

ROYAL DOULTON

Originally established at Lambeth in London, the company expanded at the end of the nineteenth century by opening a factory at Burslem in the Potteries. During, the 1930s, Charles Noake was employed as the company's Art Director. He worked together with his son, Jack, who was appointed successor to his father in 1936.

One of the first Deco inspired shapes, introduced in 1932, was the Casino shape. The shape was streamlined and simple; although, a distinctive feature of the lids to coffee pots, teapots, and tureens was a novel half circular shaped handle. Casino was available in earthenware and china. Patterns applied to the shape included Radiance, which was comprised of green banding with black hairlines, and the alternative colourway of Marquis with orange banding and brown hairlines. Other patterns used for the shape were Tango, loosely based on a sunburst, and the paisley Lynn.

The Tango pattern, together with Zodiac and De Luxe, were also available on the Fairy shape. This shape featured a slightly conical cup with an open triangular handle. De Luxe, as the name suggests, is a luxurious and sophisticated, yet simple pattern. It combines a silky green and white body diagonally divided by a black line and edged in platinum.

The Dandy shape featured an extreme teapot design with an exaggerated triangular handle and Aztec influenced lid and footrim. It is often found decorated with the Gaylee pattern, which is a bold abstract cloud design with colourful falling rain.

Royal Doulton is also well known for their range of figurines, designed by Leslie Harradine. Over 2000 figures have been issued and many exhibit an Art Deco influence. Most notable being "Angela," "The Swimmer," "The Bather," and "The Sunshine Girl."

Royal Doulton advertisement for the Dandy shape in the Gaylee pattern. *Courtesy of Royal Doulton.*

Extract from Royal Doulton catalogue showing the Casino and Fairy shapes in the Tango pattern. *Courtesy of Royal Doulton.*

Right: Figurine, "The Bather (with costume)," Model No. HN 1708, designed by Leslie Harradine, c. 1935 to 1938. *Courtesy of Royal Doulton.* $2000+.

Below: Figurines by Leslie Harradine. Left: "The Bather (without costume)," Model No. HN 687. Right: "The Swimmer," Model No. HN 1270. *Courtesy of Royal Doulton.* $1200-2000+ each.

JAMES SADLER

The firm of James Sadler and Sons Ltd. was established at Burslem in 1882. It has for many years specialised in the production of teapots, and is most famous for its novelty Racing Car Teapot. The Racing Car Teapot, allegedly based on Sir Malcolm Campbell's "Bluebird" land speed record car, was modelled by Cyril Lancaster and designed by Eddie Sadler (who at the age of 88 still works for the company). It was first introduced in 1935 and sold for 2/6d (20 cents) trade and 5 shillings retail (40 cents/ 25p), mostly at high class gift shops.

The Racing Car Teapot was very successful at the time of production and echoed the infatuation of the nation with speed. Indeed, at the time of issue, only the very rich could af-

ford a motor car and, presumably, the ownership of a Racing Car Teapot was as close to auto ownership as the majority could aspire. It is an item that is now extremely collectible and enjoys an almost fanatical following. The design is a masterful combination of functionality and caricature.

The first few Racing Car Teapots, which are now very rare, were multi-colored and featured a green top, orange side panels, and black mudguards. These teapots were later produced in many single colors including cream, green, yellow, turquoise, blue and pink. The rarest color is black, followed by grey and brown. It is also possible to find variations of a particular color or a marbled effect to the glaze; however, these were not production colors. Such

A group of Sadler Racing Car Teapots. *Courtesy of Decodance.* $200-600.

variations were caused by a fluctuation in the firing temperature or the glaze reacting to the atmosphere.

The car is 9 inches in length and 4.5 inches in height, has a four cup capacity and the drivers head forms the lid. It was available in a plain glaze or with a half silver trim or full silver trim. Both trimmed versions have silver coach lines, details to the drivers head (including painted goggles), and bear a humorous number plate "OK T42" at the front and rear. The full trim version, additionally, has silvered mudguards. It was also available in a gold trim; although, this was limited to Salesman's samples.

A version to this teapot was also issued depicting Mabel Lucie Attwell's childrens' transfers. Customised versions were available for sale at specific seaside towns, where the side of the car declared that it was a present from that particular seaside resort.

The backstamp on the underside of the car, which is impressed into the pottery, usually reads "Made in England" on two lines, with "Registered No 820236" on two lines underneath. Sometimes, above this will be a printed Crown with the word "Sadler" in a printed ribbon. Various other painters marks can be found including "H" and "D".

The Racing Car Teapot's popularity today has enabled James Sadler (a firm still very much in existence) to re-issue limited editions of the teapot in blue with a silver trim and in green with a gold trim.

Whether you regard the Racing Car Teapot as an icon of kitsch or a masterly design embodying the age of speed, no one could argue that it is not Fun!!

The company also produced many other novelty teapots, including two that are particularly prized by collectors. These are the Aeroplane and the Football teapots. The Football teapot featured a handle in the form of a Football player arched backwards and dressed in various playing strips of different teams. The Aeroplane teapot was available in colors including green and yellow, and was produced for James Sadler by Sudlows, due to over demand for the racing car.

Portrait of Eddie Sadler in the mid-1930s.

A Black Sadler Racing Car Teapot. This is the rarest of the various colors. *Courtesy of Decodance.* $1000+.

A very rare Racing Car Teapot with the inscription "A Present from Crediton" on each side. This shows that the teapot was available in customised versions, for sale at various seaside resorts. *Courtesy of Decodance.* $475.

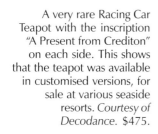

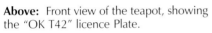

James Sadler backstamp found on the Racing Car Teapot.

Above: Front view of the teapot, showing the "OK T42" licence Plate.

Right: Limited edition re-issue of the Racing Car Teapot in British racing green with 18 carat gold trim.

TAMS WARE

John Tams Ltd. was founded in 1874 by John Tams. The company remained in family ownership until it was floated on the London Stock Exchange in 1988. Initially, they produced earthenware products for the medical sector. However, following the introduction of glass for such products, they diversified into earthenware dinnerware.

Many of their designs, were traditionally based and included such designs as the Willow Pattern. The company did, however, in the 1930s, issue a number of Art Deco inspired designs. These were released under the Tams Ware trade name and were generally quite dramatic and vivid geometrics. The designs were not dissimilar to the early geometrics designed by Susie Cooper for Grays and some are reminiscent of Myott patterns.

The limited availability of Tams Ware pieces means that a collection specifically dedicated to them will prove to be a struggle; although, they are still desirable to general Art Deco collectors.

Vase by Tams Ware, Pattern No. 1635.
Courtesy of Decodance. $350.

Above: An Octagonal Plate by Tams Ware, c. 1932. *Courtesy of Decodance.* $350.

Right: Bowl by Tams Ware in Geometric pattern, marked 1635. *Courtesy of Decodance.* $300.

Below: Tams Ware backstamp.

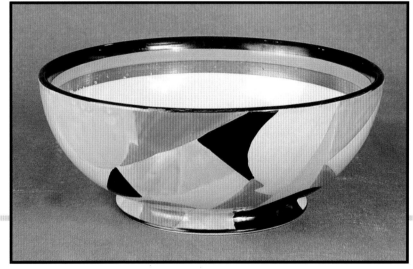

ENDNOTES

CHAPTER 1

1. Bevis Hillier, *Art Deco of the 20s and 30s* (London: Herbert Press, 1968), p. 10-12.
2. Bevis Hillier and Stephen Escritt, *Art Deco Style* (London, Phaidon Press Ltd, 1997), p. 19-25.

CHAPTER 2

1. Katherine Morrrison McClinton, *Art Deco a Guide for Collectors*.(New York:Potter, 1986), p. 116-117.
2. Graham Mclaren, *Ceramics of the 50s* (Princes Risborough, Shire Publications,1997), p. 5-7.

CHAPTER 4

1. Andrew Casey, *Susie Cooper Ceramics* (Stratford-Upon-Avon: Jazz Publications, 1992), p. 9-13.
2. Ann Eatwell, *Susie Cooper Productions* (London: Victoria and Albert Museum 1987), p. 9.
3. Andrew Casey, p. 27.
4. Bryn Youds, *Susie Cooper an Elegant Affair* (London: Thames and Hudson, 1996), p. 27.
5. Adrian Woodhouse, *Susie Cooper* (Shirland: Trilby Books, 1992), p. 46.
6. Bryn Youds, p. 66-71.

CHAPTER 5

1. Len Griffin and Louis K and Susan Pear Meisel, *Clarice Cliff The Bizarre Affair* (London: Thames and Hudson, 1989), p. 11-17.
2. Richard Green and Des Jones, *The Rich Designs of Clarice Cliff* (Bidford-On-Avon: Rich Designs, 1995), p. 24.
3. Len Griffin and Louis K and Susan Pear Meisel, p. 25.
4. Howard and Pat Watson, *The Clarice Cliff Color Price Guide* (London: Francis Joseph,1995), p. 9.
5. Peter Wentworth-Shields and Kay Johnson, *Clarice Cliff* (London: L'Odeon, 1976).

CHAPTER 7

1. Judy Spours, *Art Deco Tableware: British Domestic Ceramics 1925-1939* (London: Ward Lock,1991), p. 156.
2. Judy Spours, p. 197.

CONTACTS

ART DECO DEALERS
Decodance
(Incorporating Colin Mawston Art
      Deco Consultancy).
Tel 01233 611171.
URL: www.decodance.com.
E.Mail: decodance@yahoo.co.uk

Banana Dance
The Northcote Road Antiques Centre
155a Northcote Road
London SW11 6QB   England
URL:www.banana-dance.co.uk.
Tel:0181 699 7728

Carole A.Berk Ltd
4918 Fairmount Avenue
Bethesda   Maryland 20814   U.S.A.
U.R.L:www.caroleberk.com/collect.htm
E.Mail:cab@caroleberk.com.

Bona Arts
The Hart Shopping Centre
Fleet Hants GU13 8AZ   England
U.R.L.www.bona.co.uk.
Tel: 01252 372188

Thornhill Books
43 Thornhill Close
Houghton Regis
Bedfordshire LU5 5SG
Tel:01582 861140

St Clere-Carlton Ware
P.O.Box 161
Sevenoaks
Kent TN15 6GA England
E.Mail:stclere@ao1.com

COLLECTORS CLUBS
Carlton Ware Collectors International
P.O. Box 161
Sevenoaks
Kent TN15 6GA England
Tel:01474 853630
E.Mail:cwciclub@aol.com

Clarice Cliff Collectors Club
Fantasque House
Tennis Drive
The Park
Nottingham NG7 1AE   England

Society Art Deco Victoria
P.O.Box 1324 Collingwood
Victoria 3066   Australia
Tel:(03)9428 0519

Detroit Area Art Deco Society
C/o Thomas Rusinow
22808 Sherwood
Warren MI48091-2696   U.S.A.

The Shelley Goup
12 Lilleshall Road
Clayton
Newcastle-under-Lyme
Staffordshire ST5 3BX   England

Art Deco Society of California
100 Bush Street
511 San Francisco
CA 94104982   U.S.A.

Auckland Art Deco Society
P.O.Box 109-304
Newmarket
Auckland   New Zealand
Tel:(64)9620 7484
URL:www.auckland.net.nz/artdeco

ART DECO FAIRS
Deco Fairs
BM. Deco
London WC1N 3XX   England
Tel: 0181 663 3323

Midland Art Deco Fairs
Tel:0121430 3767

PUBLICATIONS
Deco Echoes
P.O. Box 155
Cummaquid
M.A. 02637   U.S.A.
Tel:1.8006955768
URL:www.deco-echoes.com

The Agora (Clarice Cliff)
G. Stater
P.O. Box 3503
Western ACT 2611   Australia

AUCTION HOUSES
Bonhams
65-69 Lots Road
Chelsea
London SW10 0RN   England
URL:www.Bonhams.com
E.Mail:j.mccall@bonhams.com
Tel:0171 393 3900

Sotheby's
34-35 New Bond Street
London W1A 2AA   England
Tel: 0171 493 8080
URL:www.sothebys.com

Sotheby's
Summers Place
Billinghurst
West Sussex RH14 9AO
Tel:01403 833500

Gardiner Houlgate
The Old Malt House
Comfortable Place
Upper Bristol Road
Bath   England
Tel: 01225 447933

Phillips-Selkirk
7447 Forsyth Boulevard
St Louis
MO 63105   U.S.A.
Tel: 3147265515

INTERNET SITES
Clarice Cliff Collectors Club
www.claricecliff.com/

Susie Cooper Museum
www.hsnt.or.jp/~okabe/susie.html
E.Mail:keiko@hsnt.or.jp

E. Bay On-Line Auctions
www.ebay.com/

Latimores Art Deco Directory
www:/latimore.co.uk

Shelly Group
www.shelley.co.uk/

Decodance.
www.Decodance.com.

BIBLIOGRAPHY

BOOKS

Calvert, Helen. *Collecting Chameleon Ware.* Atglen, Pennsylvania: Schiffer Publishing, 1998.

Casey, Andrew. *Susie Cooper Ceramics: A Collectors Guide*, Warwickshire, England: Jazz Publications Ltd., 1992.

Collecting Susie Cooper, London: Francis Joseph Publications, 1994.

Coupe, Elizabeth. *Collecting Burleigh Ware.* England: Coupe, 1998.

Coupe, Elizabeth. *Collecting Burleigh Jugs.* England: Coupe, 1998.

Cunningham, Helen. *Clarice Cliff and her Contemporaries.* Atglen; Schiffer, 1999.

Curtis, Tony. *Art Deco Ceramics.* London: Lyle, 1999.

Davenport, Chris. *Shelley Potteries The Later Years.* England: Heather Publications, 1997.

Durrant, Stuart. *Christopher Dresser.* London: Academy Editions, 1993.

Eatwell, Ann. *Susie Cooper Productions.* London: Victoria And Albert Museum, 1987.

Green, Richard, and Des Jones. *The Rich Designs of Clarice Cliff.* Warwickshire, England: Rich Designs, 1995.

Griffin, Len. *Clarice Cliff: The Art of Bizarre.* London: Pavilion, 1999.

Griffin, Leonard and Louis K., and Susan Pear Meisel. *Clarice Cliff: The Bizarre Affair.* London: Thames and Hudson, 1995.

Haywood, Leslie. *Poole Pottery.* Somerset, Richard Dennis, 1995.

Hill, Susan. *The Shelley Style.* Stratford-upon-Avon: Jazz, 1997.

Hillier, Bevis and Stephen Escritt. *Art Deco Style.* London: Phaidon Press Ltd., 1997.

Hillier, Bevis. *Art Deco of the 20s and 30s.* London: Herbert Press, 1968.

Knowles, Eric. *100 Years of the Decorative Arts.* London: Millers, 1998.

Knowles, Eric and Judith and Martin Miller. *Art Nouveau & Art Deco Buyers Guide.* England: Millers, 1995.

McClinton, Katherine Morrison. *Art Deco A Guide For Collectors.* New York: Potter, 1986.

McCready, Karen. *Art Deco And Modernist Ceramics.* London: Thames & Hudson Ltd., 1995.

McLaren, Graham. *Ceramics Of The 1950s.* Pembrokeshire, England: Shire Publications, 1997.

Niblett, Paul. *Hand-Painted: Gray's Pottery.* Stoke-on-Trent: City Museum and Art Gallery, 1982. Reprint, 1983, 1987.

Serpell, David. *Collecting Carlton Ware.* London: Francis Joseph, 1999.

Spours, Judy. *Art Deco Tableware: British Domestic Ceramics 1925-1939.* London: Ward Lock, 1991.

Stevenson, Greg. *Art Deco Ceramics.* England: Shire, 1998.

Watson, Howard. *Collecting Clarice Cliff.* London: Kevin Francis Publishing, 1988.

_____, and Pat. *Collecting Art Deco Ceramics.* London: Kevin Francis Publishing, 1993.

_____. *Collecting Art Deco Ceramics.* 2nd, ed. London: Francis Joseph Publications 1997.

_____. *The Clarice Cliff Color price Guide.* London: Francis Joseph Publications, 1995.

_____. *The Colorful World of Clarice Cliff.* London: Kevin Francis Publishing, 1992.

Wentworth-Shields, Peter, and Kay Johnson. *Clarice Cliff.* London: L'Odeon, 1976.

Woodhouse, Adrian. *Susie Cooper.* England: Trilby Books, 1992.

Youds, Bryn. *Susie Cooper: An Elegant Affair.* London: Thames and Hudson Ltd., 1996.

CATALOGUES, JOURNALS AND MAGAZINES

Clarice Cliff Quarterly Reviews, Clarice Cliff Collectors Club

Clarice Cliff and British Decorative Arts Auction Catalogues, Christies

Clarice Cliff Auction Catalogues, Bonhams.

Christopher Dresser Exhibition Catalogue, June 1999, New Century.

World Of Art Deco Exhibition Catalogue, 1971, Bevis Hillier For The Minneapolis Institute of Arts.

EAST BATON ROUGE PARISH LIBRARY

3 1659 02209 8962

**EAST BATON ROUGE PARISH
LIBRARY**
BATON ROUGE, LOUISIANA

DISCARD

MAIN

2000